Praise for *Why Your Weird.*

I love Laurie Wallin's heart and her simple, yet profound message. This is a gem of a book that'll coach you toward living the life you've always wanted but were afraid to try.

—**Mary DeMuth**, author of 15 books including
The Wall Around Your Heart

Laurie is an encourager of the heart. She knows what women need to hear and says it in a way that makes receiving her words a joy. Let her come alongside you through these pages and walk with you where Jesus wants you to go!

—**Holley Gerth**, author of the best-selling book
You're Made for a God-Sized Dream

If you ever wondered why you don't quite fit in, this book is for you. Laurie takes you on a journey that says don't change what God has masterfully crafted together. She illustrates that imperfection is brilliant—so celebrate your weirdness! When you read this book you will get a new perspective of how uniquely beautiful each person is and how much people need what you have to give.

—**Craig Johnson**, Director of Ministries, Lakewood Church,
author of *Lead Vertically*

Why Your Weirdness is Wonderful helped me to rethink my life, my purpose, who I have been, who I am, and who I can be. Life circumstances can affect us deeply, detour us, cause us to lose our way, or simply forget who we are. This book is a great tool that can help you to find your way back to who God designed you to be. I highly recommend it!

—**Karla Hoelscher**, church planter

Like wearing clothing that belongs to someone else is how we must look when we don't embrace the strengths and weaknesses God has given us.

Laurie asks all the right questions as a great conversationalist and teacher—to guide us on the journey to relationship with God as we discover our own personal treasures and realize "The Lord will accomplish what concerns me" (Ps. 138:8)! Expect to be energized and excited as you begin to exhibit the wonderful ways God made you to be!

—**Cindi Ferrini**, national speaker with FamilyLife,
author of *Balancing the Active Life*

God enjoys you just as you are right now—with all of your shortcomings and quirks. In *Why Your Weirdness Is Wonderful*, Laurie Wallin not only provides us with a new lens through which to view our uniqueness but also helps us excavate our gifts and strengths. Laurie joyfully encourages us to see ourselves through God's eyes. And what a lovely view it is. Dive into this insightful book and be filled with hope, knowing that you are a one-of-a-kind masterpiece.

—**Linda Breitman**, speaker, author of *The Real You:
Believing Your True Identity*

Every woman needs a coach to spur her on when the daily marathon of caring for young children, feisty teens, or aging parents becomes more than she can handle. In *Why Your Weirdness Is Wonderful*, author Laurie Wallin is that coach. She encourages readers to accept their strengths and weaknesses, discover the race God has for them to run, and then move forward step by step.

—**Jolene Philo**, author of *Different Dream Parenting*

If you've ever felt like you don't measure up, read this book! Laurie's writing style is conversational yet kick-in-the-pants. I was brought to tears more than once by God's passion for us and His desire to see us healthy, joyful, and whole! With lots of instructions for how to take the "next step," you won't finish this book unchanged unless you choose not to act!

—**Jennifer A. Janes**, wife and mom; homeschooling
and special needs blogger

WHY YOUR WEIRDNESS
Is Wonderful

EMBRACE YOUR QUIRKS & LIVE YOUR STRENGTHS

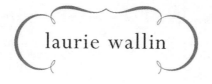

laurie wallin

ABINGDON PRESS

NASHVILLE

WHY YOUR WEIRDNESS IS WONDERFUL
EMBRACE YOUR QUIRKS AND LIVE YOUR STRENGTHS

Copyright © 2014 by Laurie Wallin

Library of Congress Cataloging-in-Publication Data

Wallin, Laurie.
  Why your weirdness is wonderful : embrace your quirks and live your strengths / Laurie Wallin.
    pages cm
  Includes bibliographical references.
  ISBN 978-1-4267-7200-9 (binding: soft back, pbk. : alk. paper) 1. Self-esteem—Religious aspects—Christianity. 2. Self-acceptance—Religious aspects—Christianity. I. Title.
  BV4598.24.W35 2014
  248.4—dc23

2013038413

14 15 16 17 18 19 20 21 22 23—10 9 8 7 6 5 4 3 2 1

MANUFACTURED IN THE UNITED STATES OF AMERICA

*To my husband, whose insights and humor have kept me sane
through fifteen years of challenges. And to my children,
who shared their mom with these pages for six months.
I love each of you more than you know, quirks and all.*

Contents

PART I

YES, YOU'RE WEIRD—BUT IT'S A GOOD WEIRD

Wonder is the precondition for all wisdom.
—Christian Wiman, My Bright Abyss

IMAGINE IT'S YOUR BIRTHDAY. You're all dressed up, enjoying lunch with a friend. After the plates are cleared, she passes you the shiny wrapped box. She grins and says, "Open it! I saw this, and it was so perfect I couldn't resist."

You yank off the bow, tear away the paper, open the box . . . and find a strange item inside. *What is it?* you wonder. You pull it out and turn it in your hands. You're pretty sure it's supposed to be a good thing—it is a gift from a dear friend, after all. Confused, you smile and thank her. Savoring the friendship and the mocha cheesecake, you finish lunch and head home where, still perplexed, you stow the box in the closet.

Maybe this has never happened to you with a birthday gift from a friend. But I'm willing to bet it's happened with a different gift. Rather than a trinket in a box, perhaps it looked more like one of these:

- You have the gift of storytelling but also wonder whether people think you talk too much.
- You have the gift of being able to think of thirty great ideas for a project but can't start or finish enough of them.
- You have the gift of keeping things predictable and orderly, but when your family doesn't behave that way, you feel angry and resentful.
- You have the gift of keeping the peace in your family or workplace but can't make peace with your thoughts or worries.
- You have the gift of supporting and encouraging people just by being there, but you sometimes feel as if you haven't accomplished enough.

- You have a gift for organizing and planning events or projects, but your tendency toward running the show annoys your spouse to no end.
- You have the gift of capitalizing on opportunities as they arrive, but you struggle, knowing people see that as being flaky or lacking direction.

"Wait a second," you may be saying, "those don't sound like gifts to me!"

They didn't to me, either. And I've wrestled with most of them over the years: things I do well, but they don't seem to be strengths to other people. And weird things I wish I'd stop doing—ways I wish I'd stop being—that just keep coming back to bite me:

- When I interact with people, my brain compiles a mental Rolodex of their strengths, struggles, hopes, and needs. It makes me good at individualizing sessions as a life coach, but I can come off as spacey or, in the worst cases, uninterested when I'm in groups.
- I have a knack for influencing others. This makes me a good grant writer, an effective speaker, and a good PR person for events. When I'm tired or stressed, though, it takes on more of a used car salesperson flare (ahem).
- I am a finisher. Give me a project, and it will get done. But give me a novel while on vacation, and if I can't finish it quickly, I stress myself out. I'll be thinking about it the whole time I'm looking at Michelangelo's *David*, or I'll ignore my family for a day to finish it. I'm learning which are good times to be a book hermit at home and which are not. And I bring magazines instead of books on vacation now!

What if I told you that all those things about us—the wonderful *and* the weirdness—are gifts? What if you could sit at lunch with God, hold those quirky, challenging tendencies about you in your hands, and say, "Oh! I love these too!"

What if who you are right now is exactly who God meant you to be? What if the weirdest, most annoying things about you exist on purpose— for a purpose—to bring life, joy, strength, and healing to this world?

Whether you think I'm right or you think I'm nuts, I hope you'll join me on this journey to discover the gifts in you that quite possibly are the most valuable. Let's pull them off the shelf and see what God can do with them, shall we?

1

To Question Our Quirks

T HE IDEA THAT GIFTS EXIST in you that you've never
noticed (or maybe even forcefully rejected) may seem strange,
or even wrong. You might be thinking, *How could these tendencies possibly be OK? Why did God design me like this? I struggle every
day with [insert area of weakness here].*

Every day I hear thoughts like these from friends and clients: laments
about how they relate to God and to the world. They overthink issues,
worry too much, put things off, argue too much, talk too much, or have
any number of other grievances. They fight who they are and beg God
to make them different. They mistakenly interpret Scripture, such as the
verse that says "those who lose their lives because of me will find them"
(Matthew 10:39). They think it means *I need to stop being the way I am
so I can be more of who God intends me to be or do more of what God
has purposed me to do.* This often comes out sounding like, "God, please
make me more like [insert name of friend you think is perfect]."

Why is this?

Authors Albert Winseman, Donald Clifton, and Curt Liesveld say
it's because we've grown up with the "weakness prevention" model,
which tells us that to become strong and successful we must correct our

5

weaknesses, develop our areas of nontalent. Then we will be ready to fully serve God and the world.

We've all struggled with this ideology—focusing not on our strengths but on our weaknesses—in some form. The idea stems from the school-age question: *What about me is OK, and what isn't?* What began as a simple desire we had as kids to understand ourselves, others, and the basic truths of the world became tangled in mixed messages and experiences of loss. Then it twisted into a deep source of pain and shame when we started to assign words like *wrong* and *bad* to how we naturally relate to life and people.

I see this happen often in my daughters' hearts as they progress through school. Most recently my seven-year-old announced, in one of our bedtime-foot-rub moments, that her friends don't like her because she gets better grades on certain assignments than they do. She'd started getting poor grades in math (her favorite subject) in the month leading up to that conversation, so I took a risk and asked, "Any chance you're doing the work poorly so they'll like you more?"

A long silence. Then her sweet, quiet, honest "maybe" opened the door for us to figure out how she could enjoy achieving in her favorite subject and encourage the other girls: she could offer to help them, learn how to change the subject, or ask to move seats and ignore their remarks.

You and I were created in the image of God. And God says our design is "supremely good."

Whatever we came up with, the point was to separate her tendency to work hard and effectively with numbers from the judgment of her "friends" at school, because there's no way this mama was going to let any ponytail diva attack my kid's love for learning! (Did I mention another of my quirks is that I get passionate about things? This has obvious use—and probably more obvious pitfalls.)

You're not my seven-year-old, but like her, you and I were created in the image of God. And God says our design is "supremely good" (Genesis 1:31). You and your overthinking, overplanning, worrying, quirky self were made on purpose to reveal God to the world around you in a way only you can do.

In your weirdness. Not in spite of it.

How does that work? We find the answer in Scripture, where Paul (a guy with major weirdness issues that we'll discuss later) writes the message God gave him: "'My grace is enough for you, because power is made perfect in weakness.' So I'll gladly spend my time bragging about my weaknesses so that Christ's power can rest on me" (2 Corinthians 12:9). "Weakness," as translated from the original Greek, refers to our inabilities as frail humans, not our wayward desires or tendencies, as some would have us believe.

And then there's that scary little word: *perfect*. It isn't the same as *flawless*, as we might be tempted to read—and as we often think God expects us to be. Nowhere in the Bible does the idea of perfection, paired with humanity, mean "faultless." It means "complete." Truly, "in God we live, move, and exist," and "without me," Jesus said, "you can't do anything" (Acts 17:28; John 15:5). In God we are complete. Lacking nothing. Perfect. Not in spite of our weaknesses, in them. It's a completion that God breathes into us by divine power.

It's in our weakness, in our weirdness, that God's completeness and power exist. When God is in our tendency to overthink, overanalyze, overplan, get too emotionally wrapped up in life, and constantly think about the future (or never think about it), God's strength shines brightest and purpose unfolds most clearly. The overthinking becomes strategic planning. The worrier's tendency to stew over eventualities becomes prayer over possibilities. The chatty one becomes the connector in a group or the one who introduces souls to Christ. The one who doesn't much consider the future becomes the one who reveals to us worrywarts the joy and beauty of this moment.

WHY YOUR WEIRDNESS IS WONDERFUL

You see, God doesn't want to work around you or your quirks. He wants to work *through* you—through them.

It isn't a matter of God's overriding our weaknesses. Instead, God uses our natural design, pouring strength through our quirks.

It's in our weakness, in our weirdness, that God's completeness and power exist.

As this happens, the weird, annoying, frustrating things about us—the things we've perhaps seen as problems or struggled against for years—become the window through which the power of God can shine brightest. Not because God removes them or "heals" us from who we are, but because God empowers us to live as who we are, only better, stronger. It's what a personal trainer would do with one of our weaker muscles: rather than perform a muscle transplant, he would use weights and exercise to show us how that part's supposed to work.

In the past few years as a life coach, I've seen this truth play out in lives again and again. As clients discover God's strength folded into their weaknesses and quirks

- marriages are healed and spouses begin to see God's design in their mates' infuriating quirks;
- ministries come to life as people accept who God has made them to be, and they let God's design make their ministry personal and more effective;
- parents find new energy, confidence, and efficacy;
- clients leave jobs that drained them for better ones or re-create current jobs to better complement who they are;
- organizers discover the peace that comes with keeping their environments—and their thoughts and feelings—arranged in helpful ways;

- highly responsible people discover how to master this trait instead of letting it master them;
- worriers invest their anxiety in prayer and see miracles happen;
- communicators who tend to gossip find ways to spread encouragement and information instead, catalyzing blessing in their neighborhoods.

In every case, clients tell me that one of the biggest wins of our working together is that they can now look in the mirror and recognize the value in their weaknesses and quirks. And that, on a good day, they're even grateful for them because they're starting to see God actively at work in their lives in these areas.

These amazing people accomplish all this as they decide to stop fighting the qualities God created in them and instead start asking:

- If I'm made in your image, God, what aspects of you am I meant to reflect?
- For what purpose did you make me this way?
- How do *you* reveal these attributes—these tendencies that seem weak in me—in a holy, grace-filled way?
- Would you please fill my weaknesses with your life and power to replace the brokenness and frustration they often bring now?

It can be a scary shift to stop fighting yourself and start following God, not just in spite of but because of a weakness: to start letting God cultivate those traits as the openings for strength they were always meant to be in you. This change in perspective may even feel as if you're walking straight into darkness and away from all you thought you understood about character. But if you've struggled to find the light in an aspect of yourself that's been tough to understand or manage, perhaps it's time to try a new approach. After all, "the quickest way for anyone to reach the sun and the light of day is not to run west, chasing after the setting sun, but to head east, plunging into the darkness until one comes to sunrise," according to Jerry Sittser, coauthor of *When Your Rope Breaks.*

Our weirdness, in God's hands, is wonderful.

The journey to make sense of and see value in our weirdness begins when we turn to face what we've run from for so long—when we let ourselves examine what we've begged God to remove from or change in us. The journey begins when we stop fighting and let God wield his strength through us—to lead us to the sense of purpose we all crave and to His peace that passes understanding. To discover—and fully, joyfully live—the truth that our weirdness, in God's hands, is wonderful.

Indeed, it's like seeing that strange, maybe even initially offensive gift peering out from the fresh-opened box in your hands. But getting to know its value? What power this will unleash in your life!

Ready to take the risk to discover the good that's hiding in those quirks? Let's start with a quick mental inventory. Which of your quirks do you doubt could ever have a purpose? Consider your closest friends: Which of their quirks irritate you, and how do the quirks affect your relationship? What challenges have your own weirdnesses created in those relationships?

Note: throughout the book you'll find questions to consider and engage. If you're like me, you'll need more than the margins here to do that! At the back of the book, there's extra space to write, draw, scribble, process, pray, study the Word of God, and enjoy that special place to dream.

2

To Be Loved,
Quirks and All

WEIRD: IT'S DEFINITELY NOT a name we wanted to be called in junior high. Maybe not even now as adults. The word carries a sense of oddness, quirkiness, and the accompanying social dislocation of having those qualities. Long ago, *weird* conveyed supernatural, mystical, and often frightening meaning. But *weird* isn't synonymous with *bad*. In fact, in this book, we're going to return to its original definition. A close relative of the Old English *wyrd*, its meaning was akin to the idea of worth.

Who doesn't need a little stronger sense of worth? In these busy days, spent vying with the seven billion people on earth for jobs, resources, real estate, and recognition, we can feel lost in the crowd, unimportant, isolated in the midst of the throng. The increase in school-age bullying shows our kids feel this crunch, too, this struggle for significance and clawing for control in a stressful, disenchanted world. In the building intensity of these times, we need to know that we still matter. That to someone, somewhere, we're not just known but loved intentionally, wholeheartedly, deeply. You know the way I'm talking about: the falling-in-love, time-stands-still, life-lives-in-his-smile, who-cares-if-he-chews-loudly-or-never-irons-his-shirts kind of love. Everyone wants to feel that kind of unconditional affection from someone.

You're living a love story like that today. And this book is an invitation to fall ever deeper in love. To see yourself and the people all around you in this bursting-at-the-seams planet with the same twinkle in your eyes as the One who designed you does. It's an invitation, a beckoning to discover the intrinsic worth woven into you, quirks and all. To learn to love the wonder in your divinely designed weirdness. As you do, you begin to accept the invitation to love the weirdos around you as well. We begin to live the Greatest Commandment and its runner-up (Matthew 22:37-40) with vigor as we learn to love God with all our hearts, minds, souls, and quirks and love others in their weirdness too.

> *This book is an invitation to fall ever deeper in love. To see yourself . . . with the same twinkle in your eyes as the One who designed you does.*

It's an idea shared a few years ago by best-selling author Robert Fulghum. In his book *True Love*, Fulghum described what he'd seen love to really be: "We're all a little weird. And life is a little weird. And when we find someone whose weirdness is compatible with ours, we join up with them and fall into mutually satisfying weirdness . . . true love."

The first person we discover compatible with our weirdness is the God who designed us in his image—a beautiful, glorious, strong image—an image that includes quirks. God's love overflows toward us as we reflect his design with abandon. God is a parent, after all. In us, God sees that little bit of himself. We look at our own kids and revel in the fact that they inherited our odd-looking toes or extra-big ears, and their quirks endear them to us. We love/hate those things about ourselves, but they're part of us and seeing them reflected is wordless communication and connection with our children. It's the same with God and our odd, annoying, or even quite challenging traits and tendencies. God wants to relate with us in every way he can.

And really, this relating—this love—is our whole point in life. We were designed to be loved, desired, pursued. We're told God loves us "with a love that lasts forever. And so with unfailing love," God says, "I have drawn you to myself" (Jeremiah 31:3). But life and its craziness crowd out this reality, this perspective. Author Emily Freeman, in her own search for divine love in life's noise, concluded, "Christ's pursuit of me is more important than my pursuit of anything else."

We can live on this crowded planet and do the next thing in front of us for a whole lifetime and miss it. We can pour our hearts into worthy pursuits, make a difference, raise our families . . . and miss it. And every day we can look at ourselves in the mirror, see our weirdness and quirks, and miss it. We can live entirely outside of what Paul said so clearly: "The greatest of these [investments, talents, gifts, challenges, hopes, and dreams] is love" (1 Corinthians 13:13). This love isn't just toward what's good in us; it's toward all of us. Our weird God (see chapter 16) loves us, his weirdo kids, like crazy, and it's high time we start to see in ourselves what God has always seen: that our weirdness is wonderful. And that we're loved more than we can imagine, right in the middle of it all.

How could knowing you're loved by God in both your strengths and your quirks change how you see those traits in yourself? In others?

3

To Love God—Heart, Soul, Mind (and Weirdness)

There isn't one great thing you were made to do.
There is one great God you were made to glorify.
Throughout your life, you'll do that in a million little ways.
—*Emily P. Freeman, "A Million Little Ways"*

E SAT ACROSS THE TINY coffee shop table, poring over the notebook she'd brought that day. My companion? Deb, a pastor and doctoral student whose work centered on helping people know and grow in their strengths. I'd asked her to meet once a month and coach me through discovering my strengths, then to help me learn how to coach others to do the same. She asked me questions each time—questions that got me thinking differently about my natural abilities in work, ministry, and relationships.

At one of our meetings, the conversation went like this:

Deb: So, Laurie, how do you live your strengths as you relate to God? How do strengths affect spiritual disciplines?
Me: What?

And that was that. I thought, *Why would I live my strengths around God? Our strengths and talents are for interacting with other . . . humans. Aren't they?* I needed to sit and think about that for a while. And the thinking took so long that I had to get up and get back to living my life.

For two years this question marinated in the back of my mind. It wasn't until my darkest moment as a parent that the answer started to show up. You see, one of my strengths (and quirks) is a desire to make a difference in the world. You'll hear more on the good, the bad, and the ugly parts of that later on. This quirk led me to want to adopt children. After a lot of prayer, research, and thought, that's exactly what my husband and I did. In 2004, two spunky, beautiful girls became our foster / adoptive daughters, and from the moment we met them, we knew they were meant to be our girls for good.

The younger of the two arrived with the diagnosis "failure to thrive"; it doesn't take a medical degree to get the gist of what that means. Over the next two years, we helped her reach a normal weight and growth rate for a preschooler, but then things started going downhill—this time, mentally and emotionally instead of physically.

With each new troubling behavior or symptom, my "make a difference" quirk led me to do whatever I could to help her. We embarked on years of weekly behavioral therapy and hundreds of hours in multiple hospital departments to discover what was keeping her inner growth stunted and her mood swings and toilet behaviors unresponsive to treatment. After five years of uphill battle for my little girl, it became clear we couldn't manage her the way she needed. We admitted her to a psychiatric hospital on our doctor's recommendation.

At that point, my "make a difference" trait was pretty bruised up, worn out, and discouraged. As with any deep-seated tendency, though, it drove me. I tried and tried and tried with our girl—trying to make a difference, trying to live my weirdness wonderfully—but I felt like more and more of a failure.

On the day she was due to be discharged from the hospital and return home, I sat in a tiny fluorescent-lit room, listening to the social worker. Her voice overly soothing, she listed all the time-intensive follow-up appointments my daughter would need (on top of what was already in place), and a quiet word formed on my lips: "No." The social worker's shocked look mirrored my feelings, but I said it again anyway: "No. My daughter cannot come home."

I'd held things together for years, absorbing the stress and anxiety. But the collective breath of relief felt in our home those days she'd been away opened my eyes to something I'd missed: while I couldn't (visibly) make a difference with this daughter, I could use that strength with the needs of my other kids, my husband, and myself. In that moment with the social worker, I had to hold this beaten-up trait's hand as I signed papers to release my daughter to the care of a long-term residential facility. I hoped and prayed that this painful choice would make the difference she so sorely needed and support the rest of the family better.

As I drove away from dropping off my daughter at the residential facility, as much as my mind knew this would make the most positive difference to her and the family, my heart doubted I could have any effective impact in the world at all. I fell into a yearlong depression. Packed on about fifteen pounds. Lost touch with some of my friends. Did the best I could each day with my other three kids at home, but honestly I don't remember much of that time.

God's presence seemed bleached that year. My faith remained, but as an act of the will, not an outflow of active joy. How could this happen to a family determined to love God in the purest form by loving kids orphaned by life? Hadn't we—hadn't I—been using my strengths for God all those years—the "make a difference" strength and the strengths of optimism, hard work, persistence, and belief? If I hadn't been using my strengths in God's service, then how could our child's biological sister, also ours through adoption, have grown and developed as well as she had?

17

That difficult season left me feeling disoriented, shaken to the core. I thought I'd been loving God all those years. I thought God understood that loving my daughter—helping her heal and grow—was loving him too. I thought I'd been living my strengths for God all that time.

I didn't realize until later that dark year what it could really mean to live my strengths *with* God and not *for* God (more on this in the next chapter). It was a shift that would surprise and propel me to joy I'd never expected to find in the weirdness that was me and my family.

You may not be facing these circumstances, but perhaps you've faced a situation that flipped what you knew about loving God or others on its head. Will you courageously take a moment to bring that to mind? Write down the gist of it. Hold that memory as we continue on this weird-to-wonderful journey.

4

To Live Weird with (Not for) God

T HE PHONE RANG IN THE hospital room. My husband's picture lit the screen, along with alerts from three texts he'd sent beforehand. I asked the device in my hand, "Did he miss the part where I'm in the delivery room with my friend who's having a baby?"

Between labor contractions, my longtime friend looked over at me, raised an eyebrow at my response, and nodded that I could answer it. Apparently the baby would give us a few more minutes.

I stepped outside. On the other line, instead of hearing, as anticipated, that my husband had been in a serious accident requiring the ER and lots of stitches, he said, "Honey, I was at the men's group this morning and shared some of our challenges with our kiddo. One of the guys is a missionary from South America and has seen many children healed from broken hearts and behaviors through the group's prayers. Would you give them a call and set up a time to pray with them for our family?"

Two things went through my mind: *Why is he calling me about this right now?* and *Fine. I'll call them. But only so you don't call me the next time I'm in the middle of a once-in-a-lifetime moment.* But deep down I knew why he'd called: he knew how broken I'd become about this issue and wanted to check with me before we ripped open the wound again. Good man.

I hung up and reentered the delivery room, glad to leave that conversation in the hallway and focus again on my friend and the new life she was birthing. I did make the call later that night, however, and arranged for a local couple connected with this ministry to pray for our daughter.

May I be painfully honest here? My "make a difference" trait was screaming in pain by this point. I did not think it would make one iota of difference for my daughter or our family to have someone pray for us again. I did it only so I could say I'd done everything I could for my little girl (another of my quirks: being an achiever). When that couple came to my house to pray, I sat on the couch, exhausted, thinking, *Let's just get this done. It probably won't work—it's not as if we and about a hundred other people haven't already prayed for her.* But that small, not-yet-quenched faith spark in me prompted me to ask God one more thing: "Give me one good reason this will be different from any of the innumerable other prayers spoken." (In other words, "God, I need *you* to make the difference right now.")

God didn't that night. But the next day, he did.

This couple instructed us to read through Ephesians fifty times to soak in the authority we have as believers in Christ to face down spiritual enemies. (Does fifty times sound a little excessive to you? It did to me too. So I didn't do it. I just read it a few times. Fortunately, God was in the mood to give me more than one gift.)

The next afternoon, I sat next to my daughter at the residential facility. We talked and played a board game, and I pressed back tears and depression—the usual. I mean, it seems like an innocuous interaction, right? Sitting and snuggling your child, playing a game? But doing it there was just wrong. For one thing, from behind thin walls we heard the anguish of mental brokenness, cries of troubled children and teens in other units. It was this alternate reality, a warped movie set, that screamed, "You're a failure, Laurie! If you'd only tried blah, blah, blah . . . your girl never would have ended up here!"

Feeling at a loss that day, I fell back on another of my weirdnesses: perfectionism. I wanted to pray for her while we visited, just to say I had handled the mom-visiting-broken-daughter moment right. I started praying the usual ways: asking God to protect, heal, and strengthen my daughter.

Then I felt God whisper to me, "I want to work *with* you, not instead of you, in prayer."

What? I thought. (I'm slow that way. See conversation with Deb in chapter 3.)

I felt God was pushing me to pray as if we were healing her together. Like a team. Instantly, my energy level grew. I'm a doer, and God was asking me not to ask him but to do something with him. To roll up my sleeves and listen to his lead and speak words of life to my daughter. It was exhilarating. Active. Alive. A prayer that had been "please heal her" changed as I sat next to her, confronting the dark places of her life and heart. I prayed, "In the name of Jesus, I speak healing, courage, power, and wholeness over you, right now and into eternity."

In that instant I started to see what it is to live my strengths—and my quirks—*with* God, not for him. God used my perfectionist motives to open the door for him to work with me and for my daughter in prayer. God knows I'm an active (impulsive?) person, and he took hold of that and focused it on my daughter and her spiritual situation. I'm a passionate (overly emotional?) woman and mother—someone who will fight hard against injustice—and God used that quirk to help me pray Scripture and truths about God's power and passion for my little girl's life. And that wounded "make a difference" strength? Even though I couldn't point my finger at exactly what I made a difference in that day, my spirit somehow knew I did.

You see, God knows me—strengths and quirks—and God invited all of me to work with him for my daughter. God invited me to get up in prayer and get moving, to look through Scripture for promises to pray on my daughter's behalf, to listen to God's quiet voice in my heart, and to say what came to mind—words that I'd never have thought of on my own but that I could see were meaningful to my daughter by the way she relaxed in my arms or breathed a quiet sigh of relief.

That one moment changed my understanding of God and how God wanted to relate to me, work with me, instead of around who I am. It set me on a path to find out what I'd been missing in this faith journey, and how I—how each of us—might be more cherished by and important to God than I'd ever imagined.

That realization grew stronger over the months that followed. Not long after this experience with my daughter, I read William Paul Young's novel *The Shack*. The book presented a game-changing idea: life is all—and I mean all—about relationship with God.

Young expresses this idea in the most captivating, understandable ways I've ever read. In his book, Mack, the main character, meets the Father, Son, and Holy Spirit face-to-face. During a conversation with Jesus, Mack—a father grieving his young daughter's tragic death—asks how people could ever move past what keeps them stuck in life. Jesus responds, "[By doing] what you're already doing, Mack—learning to live loved [by God]. . . . We're meant to experience this life, your life, together, in a dialogue, sharing the journey. You get to share in our wisdom and learn to love with our love."

That's exactly how God wants to be with us. He created each of us with strengths—the valued versions and their quirky, upside-down versions—and wants through those to love others and impact the world. As Young wrote,

God loves participation, never does anything without it. He doesn't use us as tools, he relates, co-creates with us. . . . Who you are as a human absolutely matters in this participation. When you try to be someone else, it stops revealing the character of God. It takes a billion people to start to get a glimpse of the composite character of God.

You see, God enjoys your talkative, sometimes-too-loud style. God loves that you're analytical and precise and that everything needs to be in a certain place. The Father loves that you're shy and spend about four times as much time thinking as talking (even if your husband hates that about you). God recognizes both sides of your strengths and "weaknesses" and appreciates them all as a single package—a package that God designed and wrapped—and God wants you to live all of it hand in hand with him.

Which of your quirks do you doubt God could love, let alone want you to express with him?

5

To Feed Your
Best Weirdness

IN HIS BOOK *WAKING THE DEAD: The Glory of a Heart Fully Alive*, John Eldredge maintains that truly living and loving others happen when we stop fighting ourselves and start lining up with God's heart for who we are. He writes, "You cannot love another person from a false self. You cannot love another while you are still hiding. How can you help them to freedom while you remain captive? You cannot love another unless you offer [him or her] your heart."

We can't really love people if we're not being real, being fully alive in who God made us to be. We can't do the will of the Father if we're wasting energy fighting who we are. It's the principle of the two wolves, as shared in the old Cherokee story. In it, an aging grandfather tells his grandson of his internal battle with two wolves—his tendency toward evil and his longing for goodness. After explaining this conflict, the aging man confides, "Sometimes it is hard to live with these two wolves inside me, for both of them try to dominate my spirit."

> *We can't do the will of the Father if we're wasting energy fighting who we are.*

His grandson, listening deeply, asks, "Which one wins, Grandfather?" His grandfather replies, smiling, "The one I feed."

We're feeding the wrong wolf when we focus our energy on fighting ourselves or on trying to be someone different from who God made us. When we put our energy into what not to be, we're falling into the mental trap of negativity bias—the process by which our minds naturally give negative information more weight than positive. For example, when we're dieting and we say, "I will not eat that doughnut. I will not eat that doughnut," then, of course, we eat the doughnut (and maybe one or two more) because it becomes the center of our thinking. Not only will we fail to become less weird by that process; we're going to get weaker.

So stop fighting.

And start feeding the right thing.

We can be our God-designed, weird selves in life-giving ways as we fulfill this mandate: "Adopt the attitude that was in Christ Jesus" (Philippians 2:5). This begins to happen as we make four choices.

First, we get real. By this I mean, we see things as they truly are. What made Christ's attitude one we need to emulate? Its basis on truth. In the original language, "attitude" comes from the Greek *phroneō*, which means "to have understanding, be wise, have a modest opinion of self." Jesus saw himself correctly, and we need to as well. When we see ourselves clearly—our gifts, our strengths-disguised-as-weirdness, our God-given tendencies—we can begin to see God use our quirks for good.

Second, we need to starve the unhelpful versions of our weirdness. We notice when the uglier sides of our quirks pop up, acknowledge those tendencies, and turn the other way because ultimately the negative side of our weirdness is like a toddler testing limits. We handle our kids' annoying behaviors by teaching them what's right, offering consequences when they stray, and nurturing the behaviors and mind-sets that are best for them. We can do this for ourselves too. When we notice we're overthinking a situation, we can ignore the life-draining version of our hyperfocus and choose to overthink on a verse of Scripture instead. When we get demanding and bossy, we can pray boldly and in the authority of our position in Christ and boss the spiritual forces of darkness back to their rightful place. Starve the negative; feed the positive.

Third, we flaunt what is good. Like Kate, the duchess of Cambridge, who while pregnant dressed in Jackie O–style dresses that showed off her fit legs and minimized her just-like-the-rest-of-us belly well into the third trimester. If we wear clothes that highlight our best features, why don't we show off our best internal traits in the same way? Why not volunteer for jobs at church that match what we're great at instead of what we think we *should* do, for example? Once I started looking at my quirks this way, when I had the choice between being the emcee of a women's event and working in the nursery, I grabbed that microphone and hammed my chatty way right through the weekend, using my quirks to make people laugh and feel comfortable and to weave the weekend's theme through each talk or activity. Big win for everyone, especially the nursery kids! No offense, nursery lovers, it's just that I wasn't born with that gene.

Fourth, we invite God to change our minds. God is the only one who can truly do this. We're stuck in this "dead corpse" of fallen humanity (Romans 7:24), but God offers wisdom freely when we ask (James 1:5). We can stop fighting and trust that when our thoughts are a mess, God will lead us out of confusion. How does that work? When we're feeling stressed about some way we respond or act, we need to stop and look up. We can ask God right then, "What do you want me to do with this weirdness? Because I know there's a right way to handle this, no matter what I'm facing or feeling." God won't leave you stranded in those moments, friend. So look up and expect the help that God promises.

As we've seen, the battle isn't against an aspect of who we are—it's not against our innate makeup. It's against faulty thinking, faulty focus, and faulty action. This is why so much of the Bible emphasizes how we think, how we perceive, and how we process what we know as life. When we make the shift from thinking our quirks, tendencies, and styles are bad and start to see that good or bad rests only in how we use those attributes, abundant life begins.

What negative view of yourself or your traits could you choose to starve today? Which beneficial one might you feed a little more?

PART II

OPENING THE DOOR
TO WONDERFUL

One rarely knows where to begin . . . though by necessity,
we can only start where we are.
—*Anne Lamott,* Stitches

EXCITEMENT WOUND ME UP so much I'd barely slept the previous night. I couldn't wait to be in the room with them—to speak to the women who'd come for the meeting, helping them connect with more of God's vision for them and move nearer to their dreams. But that morning, when I looked out at their beautiful faces and asked, "What are you great at?" I saw blank stares. Some actually shook their heads as if to say, *Nope. Can't think of anything.*

You know that screechy tire sound when a car slams on the brakes to avoid an accident? I'm pretty sure I heard that sound in the room that morning. As any coach would do when silence hits, I asked more questions: "What makes you unique? What are you known for? What do you love to do?"

Their struggle visible, one brave woman finally spoke: "It's silly, but ..."

My cheeks flushed hot. Not because her comment was goofy or wrong, but because I was mad! I ranted to myself, *Nobody can think of what she's great at? And the one who does labels it "silly"? Hold me back, people.*

Somehow life had led them to believe a lie: that when God was doling out aspects of his image in each of us, they'd gotten a dud, if anything. My heart ached over this. I wondered how long they'd been missing out on something precious: the amazing, unique, and crucial persons God designed them to be.

Even more, if they couldn't recognize or articulate what they were great at, they were missing the key to what they were meant to do with their lives. If they couldn't see that first step, how would they live their purpose ... their dreams?

That day, my prepared talk went out the window, and we spent forty minutes as a group mining hearts for the good that God had woven into each of the women there, finding evidence of how those traits had affected their lives and communities positively, and looking for ways to live the wonder in their weirdness more intentionally. I hope you'll join me in that same process here.

Somehow life had led them to believe a lie: that when God was doling out aspects of his image in each of us, they'd gotten a dud, if anything.

This section shares stories and principles that help us take the first steps toward (re)discovering our strengths and getting to know the value in our quirks.

6

WRESTLING WITH QUIRKS

THOSE PRECIOUS WOMEN WHO couldn't verbalize their strengths and quirks aren't alone. It's a struggle that's happening in every one of us, in many ways. This fact smacked me over the head when I least expected it a few months after that event.

It had been a typically long day for this writer-coach-mama with dishes piled too high in the sink. I opened my laptop to read some favorite authors' blogs. With a fresh mug of hot cocoa in one hand and an eighty-pound Labrador retriever attempting to curl up in my lap, I could feel the day's tension releasing.

Until I came across a blog post that hijacked my happy place.

Now, let me preface this by saying how much I admire this post's author, Mary DeMuth. As a fellow speaker and writer, she has encouraged me, and she lives up to her website's theme of helping people live uncaged by their pasts, worries, and fears. But even the most functional, successful people battle the "I've got a dud trait" idea, a truth Mary's post drove home that day. She'd titled it "Oh That Pesky Overactive Conscience." The post shared the history of her struggle with overthinking things and some of the life circumstances that led to this pattern. Toward the end of the post, she concluded with these words: "So maybe, just maybe, I'll learn to rest in Jesus' grace. Maybe I'll let go of my hyperactive conscience and better rely on the Holy Spirit. I hope so. I think it will mean more freedom."

Having talked on the phone with her a few times, I could almost hear her voicing the words. I wanted to leap through my computer screen and give her a giant "Been there!" hug. This, followed immediately by the urge to shake her by the shoulders and cry out, "Nooo!"

Before you judge me for this odd reaction, please understand. Yes, what she expressed is solid and biblical. Yes, we are to long to be more like Jesus in all areas of our lives. And, yes, there is always room for improvement in how we engage and respond to the world.

What bothered me was this: God made Mary an overthinker. That aspect of her isn't a dud. It reflects something about God's nature. Or at least, that's what it is supposed to do. God thought of Mary long before she was ever the woman whose words we read, listen to, and share. He considered how she'd see the world, respond to it, and impact it. And God decided overthinking would be just the perfect gift to make her the Mary the world loves and needs.

Let's make it personal. That quirk you despise about yourself? It reflects something important about God's nature. At least, that's what it is intended to do. Remember chapter 1? There we saw that when God created humankind—including Mary and each one of us—we were made in the divine image in such a way that God proclaimed us *very good*.

That quirk you despise about yourself? It reflects something important about God's nature. At least, that's what it is intended to do.

Perhaps to this you'd say, "Yes, but that was before original sin. In the garden of Eden. The intention was for us to be made in God's image, but Adam—and consequently the rest of us poor schlubs—messed it up."

Does sin negate what God created? Or cause us to no longer be creations that reflect God's image? Or does it mean that everyone after Adam and Eve is accidental, not made in the design of God? Or worse, that God lost control over how we're created?

If so, what did King David mean when he said, "You . . . created my innermost parts; / you knit me together while I was still in my mother's womb" (Psalm 139:13)? Or the prophet Jeremiah, when he wrote,

> The LORD's word came to me:
> "Before I created you in the womb I knew you;
> before you were born I set you apart."
> (Jeremiah 1:4-5)

Most people would regard these as upstanding guys. David is even called—by God, no less—"a man after [God's] own heart" (Acts 13:22 NKJV). It seems from their words that God's design extends not just beyond the first sin committed by Adam and Eve in the garden but indefinitely to today.

Beyond that, doesn't Scripture affirm that what God designs is good? That God gives good gifts, treasures that make even the most loving human parent's gifts to her child seem hard as a rock (Matthew 7:11)? The Apostle Paul described some of these good gifts—given to bring blessing not just to those who receive them but to everyone affected by them: "There are different spiritual gifts but the same Spirit; and there are different ministries and the same Lord; and there are different activities but the same God who produces all of them in everyone . . . for the common good" (1 Corinthians 12:4-7).

As with many well-known passages, these verses in 1 Corinthians can be too easy to read and forget. But if we take a moment to consider each gift listed in the spiritual short list of 1 Corinthians 12 and its Romans 12 counterpart, we might find a few quirks hiding here. Let's see what God considers "good."

Prophecy (1 Corinthians 12:10): a gift that some have to understand and convey the mind of God. These people are the innovators, the ones who push us outside the box and stretch us beyond our comfort zones. They're respected, consulted, honored. And they're also sometimes called crazy, run out of town, ignored. In biblical times, they probably looked a little nuts as they talked—sometimes even argued with—the invisible God (see the book of Jeremiah as an example).

Healing (1 Corinthians 12:9): a gift that facilitates restoring health to bodies and minds. Healers are also respected, consulted, honored. Except when they don't succeed. Or when they come off as being arrogant or playing God, or when they see patients as problems instead of people. Then we want to sue them. But healing is among the gifts God gave for everyone's benefit; it can become a weakness if misused.

Service (Romans 12:7): a gift that drives its owner to support and provide resources to others. People with this gift are loved, appreciated, and breaths of fresh air in a busy world like ours. But haven't we also known helpers who lose themselves in the helping? Who become overinvolved, fixers, or maybe even controlling or what we'd call codependent? Helping is a gift that becomes a weakness when its users get off track.

Leadership (Romans 12:8): a gift that generates presence, vision, and authority. Do I even need to mention how we talk and think of people with this gift when they have a bad day? Spend two minutes reading tabloid headlines at the checkout stand if you need a refresher. Or listen to your kids talk about their teachers at school. One day, they admire the teachers' demand for their best work, but the day those teachers assign homework over spring break? No more Mr. Nice Student.

Call me nuts, but based on this gift list and David's words in the Psalms, I'm going with the theory that when God designed humans, God did it—and keeps doing it—the way God does everything else: exactly right and in a way that requires our dependence on him. Even when

Adam and Eve chose mortality and spit in God's proverbial eye, God continued to form each and every one of us in our mothers' wombs. We are designed with good gifts, all of which could go either way: good or bad. Each of our traits is an aspect of God's image, and each carries the weight of the choice: Will that tendency reveal God or tarnish God's image? We'll see how this applies to Mary DeMuth's situation—and ours—in the next chapter.

Each of our traits is an aspect of God's image, and each carries the weight of the choice: Will that tendency reveal God or tarnish God's image?

Take the list of challenging traits you compiled in chapter 1. Write down how each quirk could also be a spiritual gift based on how you use it.

7

SQUASHING WONDERLESS SELF-TALK

REGAINING COMPOSURE, I restrained myself from calling Mary DeMuth right then at 11:00 p.m. Instead, I decided to leave this comment on her post:

The one thing I wonder as I read your post and others' reactions here is this: when God says you're fearfully and wonderfully made, does that include everything BUT your drive to arrange, achieve, and consider life intensely? What if the question was less "How can I empty myself of attributes [quirks] for Jesus?" and more "How can I reveal him more fully to others THROUGH those attributes?"

Her response? Gracious, and like many others I've heard from friends and clients: "I agree to a certain extent, except for those traits that, if left unchecked, hurt us in the long run." I could see where Mary was coming from. For some folks, overthinking, making lots of lists, and having an overactive conscience can be self-destructive, so it's hard to regard these as attributes God wants us to have.

Additionally, we find wisdom again and again in Scripture that seems to speak against these tendencies. For example, we know we need to plan diligently—maybe making lists to do so—but we must trust the outcome of our plans to God since our perspective is limited (Proverbs 21:31). For those of us who naturally think, plan, and make lists, we've coined the negative term *overthinking* to describe what we're doing when we're not trusting God in our planning. That term reflects what happens when we choose to get stuck in fear, but it doesn't reflect the positive potential that resides in this trait. Because of that, a term like *overthinking* stands in the way of what's truly possible in someone with this characteristic.

What if we set aside the word for a moment and take an objective look at this tendency? What if we renamed it *full thinking*? Having removed the negative slant from that idea, let's see what's really there.

First, for Mary, does this quality ever bring benefits? My initial thought is yes, even though I don't know her beyond our professional interactions. Just from hearing her speak, reading her blog, and talking on the phone, I've benefited from how she thinks through ideas. Even more, from the way she presents those ideas: boldly, concisely, with words well chosen.

Wait a minute! That sounds like a strength called *communication*, a trait described by authors Albert Winseman, Donald Clifton, and Kurt Liesveld as one that helps people hear and connect with important ideas and information. It's a strength that "drives [the] hunt for the perfect phrase . . . [for] powerful word combinations." What bugs Mary about herself (full thinking) is part of an aspect of God's character that Mary is meant to express—her ability to communicate effectively.

In a later post, Mary shared that she recognizes communication as one of her strengths, which brings with it a need to think hard on the how and why and when of what she communicates through living, writing, and speaking. Thought of one way, full thinking is a hurtful quality; thought of from God's viewpoint, it's a gift that helps others understand more about God, the world, and themselves.

These tendencies to think, reason, and pick just the right words are part of what make Mary—and others with these tendencies—great because they reflect great aspects of God. One of the many mentions of God's wisdom, thought, and planning appears in Psalm 40:5:

> You, LORD my God!
>> You've done so many things—
>> your wonderful deeds and your plans for us—
>>> no one can compare with you!
>> If I were to proclaim and talk about all of them,
>>> they would be too numerous to count!

God's a planner and thinker too. Except that God's plans always come to pass just as designed and in ways that best aid creation. For this complex universe to come together and continue requires serious thought, planning, and execution. Even people as thoughtful as Albert Einstein and Stephen Hawking haven't grasped the entirety of it yet. Beyond that, God thinks so many thoughts about you and me that we couldn't begin to count them. In this case, overthinking—what I'd call *full thinking*—seems like a wonderful attribute indeed.

So Mary is a chip off the Old Block when it comes to thinking traits, just as each of us is with his or her traits and tendencies. When she thinks on God and Scripture, and when she conveys that full thinking—even her struggles with it—to others, it's a window to divine wisdom. It's not in spite of her thinking but because she is able to mull over ideas well that God empowers her with insight, humor, and hope that the world needs. Put simply, when God's heart powers Mary's thinking or any of her other quirks, peoples' lives get uncaged. How do I know? Because of the way they respond on her blog. And because I've seen this same phenomenon in friends and clients again and again.

Every client I've coached eventually runs up against one of her weaknesses along the way to the dream or goal she is pursuing. The ultraresponsible client struggles with negativity and resentment because other people aren't being as responsible as she assumes they should be. The client who always sees the silver lining in situations often feels unloved because in tough times friends push her joy away, making her feel irrelevant. The intense learner feels lonely in her marriage because, after a long day with the kids, she wants to read instead of relate with others.

Every single time, as we talked it through, my clients and I discovered the "weakness" they fought was one of their strengths trying to come out.

It was stories like these that led me to start an experiment in my coaching. Every time a client lamented a certain trait—some weirdness or quirk—I'd ask, "Has that annoying tendency ever been helpful to you or someone else?"

Know what? Every single time, as we talked it through, my clients and I discovered the "weakness" they fought was one of their strengths trying to come out.

Every single time.

This made our work a little easier. Instead of putting effort in two places—press into the strengths and start damage control of the weaknesses—we could squash that wonderless self-talk and focus entirely on pressing into their strengths so that they come out as the gifts God intends them to be. Just like Mary, they could begin to see their quirks, when used in a healthy way, as friends instead of enemies.

Have you seen someone's quirk also act as a gift in her life or someone else's? What benefits did that weirdness bring to the situation?

8

Letting Go of Borrowed Quirks

YOU WOULDN'T KNOW IT if you saw me speaking to a group or hanging out with friends, but sometimes I'm pretty shy. Ever since I became a mom, that retiring girl in me has become more dominant. She convinces me not to say hello to other moms at the park. She finds ways to busy me in the kitchen when friends come over. She makes excuses at church about how she needs to get the kids from Sunday school so we can go to lunch, as though the five minutes of connecting with other adults might starve my kids to death.

During a recent season of family change, I started resenting my shyness. I began to ask why I felt that way about something I'd begun to think was simply one of my quirks. Around the same time I started repainting my house, and that process helped me realize why I wasn't meshing with my shy-girl weirdness: it wasn't mine. It was a trait that belonged to my pain, a trait I'd taken on accidentally as I parented my two older girls who, in their post-foster-care brokenness threw spectacular public tantrums and falsely accused me of hurting them, drawing suspicious looks from people around us.

My shyness was a reaction to pain. It was a side effect of raising our girls amid early hurts. As I painted my house many years later, I saw how the literal scuffs and scrapes on my walls were visible reminders of what I hadn't been able to absorb into myself during the healing journey.

For the first wall I repainted, I chose the same off-white that we'd moved in to ten years earlier. It looked clean, bright, and whole again. But something in me itched for more than just getting back to what had been normal. A trip to Home Depot and a little courage later, I started rolling on bolder colors. With each new hue covering life's scuffs and scrapes with vibrance, I found myself feeling stronger. Exhilarated even.

Why? Because shyness was a false quirk of mine. It was a borrowed quirk that someone else could live well, but I wasn't wired that way. Underneath my version of shy lurked something broken and life-draining. After trying to deal with my daughters' pain, I had allowed insecurity to close me in. To tell me it was OK to back away from other people and make excuses to avoid them. To ignore my false quirk and keep my life a safe, anonymous shade of white. But I got tired of it, so much so that I decided to break up with my shyness. To take its hands off my heart and begin instead to reach out to people again. And, while I was at it, to paint my house bright and wonderful colors that reflected my deep joy in sharing life with visitors.

Insecurity happens when we're trying to live someone else's quirks.

Insecurity happens when we're trying to live someone else's quirks. Borrowed weirdness can't work wonderfully in us because it's meant for someone else.

You can break up with whatever borrowed quirks insecurity and pain have foisted on you. The process starts with two important steps.

First, soak in the truth. In my case, the truth was that I wasn't shy; I was just hiding in my pain. When I could face and put my pain aside, I could be outgoing again. We find more of this freeing kind of truth—truth that is alive, that heals and expands and strengthens us—in Scripture. God tells us, "All Scripture is God-breathed" (2 Timothy 3:16 NIV) and is "living" and "active" in our hearts and world (Hebrews 4:12). *All* Scripture. Every single word. Its truth transforms us, opens us up to life and relationships. We looked at this next verse in a previous chapter, but let's check it out again:

> I have loved you with a love that lasts forever.
> And so with unfailing love,
> I have drawn you to myself.
> (Jeremiah 31:3)

The original meaning of "drawn you" indicates not only drawing us to or toward God but also drawing us *out of* or *away from* everything else: our shyness, insecurity, or whatever borrowed trait that's trying to pin us down. As we marinate in truth like this, we can't help feeling bolder, more empowered, and more like the beautiful people God sees in us all the time!

Second, banish your inner meanie. Stop that lying voice in its tracks. The one that says, "You can't do this," "Your house is too messy to invite them over," or "It's been too long to just pick up the phone and call them." Or even worse, the one that attacks who you are physically, mentally, or emotionally. When you feel dumpy, lonely, boring, and incapable, stand in front of the mirror and announce, "No thanks, meanie. *You're* the loser. Take a hike! God made me better than that!"

God didn't give us our gifts to paint over them with someone else's. The unique tendencies in you and me are meant to shine in a hue all their own, and in so doing, bring a little more clarity to the full-color beauty of the God we reveal to the world.

What borrowed quirks have you acquired because of insecurity, fear, stress, or loss? What passages of Scripture can you use to help you let those go? How can you banish your inner meanie?

9

SEEING THE DARK
AND LIFE SIDES
OF YOUR WEIRDNESS

YOU KNOW THOSE AWKWARD introductions that happen sometimes at work or parties? The kind where someone sticks a foot in her mouth as she reaches for the handshake? ("Congratulations! When are you expecting that baby?" exclaimed to a postpartum mom is one that comes to mind.)

That's how I felt when I first interacted with a personal strengths assessment tool. Asked to take the test as part of the requirements for a leadership position I was pursuing at my church, I pored over the nearly two hundred questions on how I'd handle such and such, or whether I liked this better than that. At the end, out popped a list of five potential strengths this test suggested I had.

Instantly I realized the test was not only long but also crazy. Because there, at the top of the list, was this potential strength: significance.

This must be a mistake, I argued with the test results, which described my tendency as longing to be important in others' eyes. (Does anyone else read that as pride?)

I turned my argument toward God: *Let me get this straight. You wired me not just to be sort of talented at being prideful, but it's my top trait? How is that ever a good feature in a person?*

At that point, Guilt found scriptural ammunition and joined the discussion. She said in her prissy voice, "You're doing it all wrong. You *are* all wrong. Everything about that quirk conflicts with scriptural passages such as, 'Don't do anything for selfish purposes,' and 'Be careful that you don't practice your religion in front of people to draw their attention'" [Philippians 2:3; Matthew 6:1].

I felt like I was losing the conflict inside. I needed answers, so I interrogated myself (and God) further: *How can I balance wanting to be important to the world and wanting to honor God above it all? How do I invest in the community, help solve problems, and grow organizations the way I love to do, without getting attached to the praise of people? God, why did you make me such a freak?*

In that moment, I recalled familiar words: "My strength is made perfect in weakness" (2 Corinthians 12:9 NKJV).

I breathed the truth in and out: God's strength. *In* my weakness. Not instead of it.

Slowly, over months that followed, as I was willing to listen to my life—to pay attention to what I loved, what grabbed my interest, and whom I was most energized with—God began to show me the wonder in my weird wiring. The first step was to temporarily suspend judgment about my tendencies. No more calling them "grandiose," "overambitious," "pretentious," "proud," or any other word that cast them in a bad light.

Beyond that, I chose not to judge myself for the gravitational pull I felt toward big projects and public service. When I wanted to write a $10,000 grant to improve my middle school classroom rather than do the more routine job of grading student papers one night, I went with the grant writing. When the chance came up to assist in running my church's women's ministry versus serving in a role where I'd be behind the scenes, I went with the public role—the one where I could love and inspire people face-to-face.

Through those months of seeking God's plan for my weirdness, I prayerfully, honestly assessed what I could or couldn't do well (which is the definition of *humility*, it turns out) and acted more on what I did well than on what I thought I should do as a "good Christian woman." I found myself doing public, big-picture things for my students, friends, church, and neighborhood, and as a bonus, I had more peace and could sense God more tangibly in my life than ever before.

It turns out that I love the challenge of going after life's big fish. Doing what some would think impossible and from which some would even run in the opposite direction. Things like getting grants to outfit my low-income science classroom with enough computers and lab equipment that the superintendent brought the media to share what was possible in public schools. Or like choosing to adopt my two older daughters from foster care, despite their case being labeled *unadoptable*, because I knew God wasn't bound by a word like that.

When I saw struggling students not only passing my class but staying after school to help friends on computers provided by that grant, I thanked God for my significance quirk. Years later, when one of my older two daughters not only pressed through her early emotional challenges but also overcame them and got a math award at school, I praised God for wiring me to stick with our big-fish version of family.

Once I opened myself to the possibility that my quirk could be good, the job became mimicking God's big viewpoint instead of making myself miserable about it. God is a God who thinks big—billions-of-light-years-wide-universe big. Calm-a-raging-sea-with-a-single-word, raise-a-dead-person-from-a-grave, cast-out-legions-of-demons-from-a-soul big. When we're wired to think big, we can go with that flow in healthy, Spirit-led ways. Doing that reflects the God who made us.

The fact is, though, each of our quirks has a dark side and a life side (see the Weirdness and Wonder Cheat Sheet at the end of the book for help with this).

When our quirks are powered by self-centeredness, darkness spreads. When they're powered by God-centeredness, life and love spread.

> *When our quirks are powered by self-centeredness, darkness spreads. When they're powered by God-centeredness, life and love spread.*

How could I possibly stay away from this strength's dark side—the one powered by self-absorption, anxiety, and fear? I don't know the full answer to that yet, but from what I've seen so far, I have this gift in order to inspire people. To help them see God's bigness in ways they may never have considered—through the big fish I pursue, the big stories I share of God's heart and plans for us, and the big grace that follows colossal mess-ups along the way.

Step an inch outside magnifying God and I end up with some big, generally public meltdowns. For example, I burst into tears in the middle of a teacher staff meeting because I stayed up too late writing that grant instead of doing the "big thing" in a balanced, strategic way. Thinking big isn't a bad thing, but the why and how and when sure can be.

Having had a few of those delightful meltdowns by the time I learned the identity of my quirky strength, I knew I needed to study the significance strength at its Source. I read passages in Scripture describing the majesty, glory, big vision, and limitless love of God. Once convinced this quality was a good thing (not just a pitfall for me), I began to ask questions to guide me away from this trait's dark side and more toward its life side—the side that reflects God's heart for creation:

- What's possible in this situation?
- What's the point of pursuing this—to make myself look good or to love God and people in a big way?
- How can I best convey God's bigness in this situation?
- Is this for me to pursue, an opportunity for someone else, or simply an opportunity to pray for the situation in big, bold ways?

These types of questions invite a conversation with the One who designed us—the One who sees the weird and wonderful in each of us as one and the same. They get us out of ourselves and into what could be; they act as a sort of compass when a trait is teetering between its dark and life sides. And they can help us focus who we are toward God's best, even in our most perplexing tendencies.

Which of the questions above might unlock the life side of your quirks today?

10

TRUSTING GOD WITH
YOUR QUIRKY HEART

W E HAVE ALL KINDS OF DESIRES that shape our quirks. Our desires may be for love, friendship, healing, change, or something else entirely. What do you most long for in this season of your life? Think about it for a moment. How do you handle that desire? Do you talk about it? Do you share it with God? Do you think about it often? Do you wonder if it's even an OK desire to have?

That desire, mixed with your quirks and strengths, is worth listening to. It's another clue to your life purpose. We see that in an oft-quoted passage of Scripture from David, the boy who slew the giant and ultimately became king of Israel: "Enjoy the LORD, / and he will give what your heart asks" (Psalm 37:4).

"He will give. . . ." Did you catch that part? That's an audacious statement for David to make. After all, don't we know people who've longed for something their whole lives but never received it? What about desires in your life that seem to have been unfulfilled?

David had no shortage of opportunities to doubt God, to fear the implications of God's plans, or to be anxious about situations, and yet he knew God. David took the time to learn about God, to listen to, trust,

WHY YOUR WEIRDNESS IS WONDERFUL

talk with, believe, and love him. David delighted himself in the Lord, so his desires fell in step with God's. David trusted that even if what came his way wasn't his first choice, he could always count on God to give goodness . . . to give love. As David grew closer to God—as he grew to know God better and better—David's hopes, dreams, plans, strengths, and quirks lined up more and more with what God hoped and dreamed for him.

Because of this, David found himself living the truth we learn much later in Scripture: "When you ask me for anything in my name, I will do it" (John 14:14). And so can we. God will give what our hearts ask.

David assures us not only that God will respond to our desires but also that God will give according to them. This isn't "name it and claim it" theology. It's God's promise to us as we pursue him with our lives, and he births within us gifts, talents, quirks, and desires. When we've pulled close to God with our lives, we learn his character. God's desires become ours. God's heart becomes ours.

When we know God's character, we ask for what God would, and we can trust he will give it. It's a natural outflow of a relationship. Commentary writer Matthew Henry explains, "He has not promised to gratify the appetites of the body, and the humours of the fancy, but the desires of the renewed, sanctified soul." The renewed, sanctified soul is one that has drawn near to God and learned God's character.

Maybe you've yearned for something for a long time but have, finally and reluctantly, laid that longing to rest. For some, that rest is in and of the Lord. Thank God for it! If it's good rest, you will have peace. You may still think of that desire, since it had an important place in your heart for so long, but it will come to mind quietly, perhaps even bringing a smile or sense of relief.

This was true for me regarding one of the strongest desires I've had during my life—the desire to become a doctor. It was a career I'd proclaimed mine since I first sat in a science lesson in elementary school. I loved the idea of helping people get well and live well. Through high school, I attended summer symposiums at local medical research facilities. In college, I majored in biochemistry, took elective classes at the medical school, and volunteered in the pediatric ward at my university's hospital. During a year of study abroad in England, I was able to shadow an oncology surgeon, talk with his patients, and sit with them in the chemo rooms. My heart swelled with a sense of desire to be in this world, to love people and support them in their health, to give hope where there wasn't any.

Then after college, I went to work at a medical research lab, biding my time as I prepared for the MCAT, the qualifying exam for medical schools. Though I still got giddy attending in-service presentations from doctors at our lab meetings, over my first year I noticed the desire waning for a career in medicine. Comments from doctors at mixers about how little time they had for their patients, complaints about how insurance companies were limiting the treatment options that physicians once had—they all began to dull my view of the career. At the same time, I started noticing how much I enjoyed mentoring new lab technicians who'd joined our team after me. And how it wouldn't just be about research techniques; it would be about their lives in general.

One day I impulsively dropped by the university's teacher education department, just to see if teaching was more my thing. As I talked with advisors and other teaching students, I realized my desire for being a doctor had peacefully dropped away, and in its place a deeper desire to teach and mentor had begun to flourish. A few years later, as a teacher, I encountered coaching as a profession for the first time. The excitement I'd once felt for medicine paled in comparison to the delight I found in coaching students from low-income neighborhoods who sought to be first in their families to attend college.

If I hadn't let go of that desire for a medical career, I might never have discovered coaching. I might never have experienced the joy of helping people connect with who God designed them to be at the deepest levels. Maybe I wouldn't have written this book. It took letting go of something I'd longed for to find something better. And maybe that's true for you today in some way too.

Will you allow the Lord to keep a wound of desire open in your heart, a seed of purpose not yet sprouted, an opportunity for God to work a miracle as you delight in him?

For others, this resignation—this release of a desire—may indicate a lack of faith, a premature letting go of a divine purpose and calling, simply because we don't have the stamina to sustain hope. These desires won't let you forget. They come up in conversation or prayer, as you read books or listen to the radio. They keep knocking on your heart no matter how much you tell them to bug off. They linger over months, years even. They wake you in the night with dreams of how it will all pan out.

Perhaps now is a good time to assure you that the Lord hasn't forgotten about your heart's cravings. In fact, if you are walking in close alignment with God, he inspires them! Will you believe the truth of Psalm 37:4? Will you allow the Lord to keep a wound of desire open in your heart, a seed of purpose not yet sprouted, an opportunity for God to work a miracle as you delight in him?

What do you really want? What might God be showing you about how those desires connect to your overall purpose?

PART III

Owning the Wonder
You're Wired With

We can only be said to be alive in those moments
when our hearts are conscious of our treasures.
—Thornton Wilder

OH, HOW I LOVE MY WALKS! Fresh air. Gorgeous skies. Heart pounding with the continuous motion. But my favorite part by far is what I see on my walks: *design.*

Everywhere! Beautiful, elegant, patterned art in trees, flowers, the gauze of clouds above, and the contours of pine cones beneath. Even in the way my heart beats differently when I walk downhill versus up.

Design is just one of the marvels we can miss in our overcrowded lives. Design can take your breath away, as it does mine. Or you may need to work on honing your attentiveness and sensitivity to it—choosing to see the shapes and patterns on leaves in your yard, sitting quietly on your couch and noticing the steady, constant breathing your body does without any prompting, or hearing the steady sound of waves crashing on a shore thousands of miles from the moon that causes them. Focusing on the intricacy of God's masterful design can help dissipate the fear, the anxiety, and more than anything else, the insecurity that so easily saps the strength from our wondrous weirdness.

When we see—really see—the world around and the wonder inside us, how can we feel unimportant? How can we slip into the depths of wondering whether we matter? Or whether we're making enough of a difference?

This section delves into the intricacies and uniqueness in our design, our strengths, our quirks, and our experiences, and how we can lean into confidence because of that design.

11

Your Designer Quirks
and the Three Rs of Life

S OMETIMES I WONDER WHAT GOD is thinking. (OK, lots of times.) When prayer seems to fall fruitless to the floor, when personal battles rage unabated, and I'm frustrated with something in myself, it's easy to wonder whether God's thinking includes me at all. When I'm in one of those modes (or is that moods?)—those "Nobody loves me. I'm no good. Might as well curl up and succumb to the bag of chips" frames of mind—I often end up going on one of my nature strolls.

Enter the humble pine cone. So easily kicked to the side of the street as I walk, it reveals a pattern that's repeated in one way or another just about everywhere within the universe. A pattern of spirals, based on numbers, named for a thirteenth-century mathematician who first discovered them. These Fibonacci numbers form repetitive patterns in much of nature—from galaxies to ocean waves, from pine cones to the contour of your ear.

That's right, we carry that design motif too. On our bodies. Inside them. And it's all around us. Because we're part of God's grand design. You and I were worth fashioning. Our lives, our work, and our presence here matter more than we can imagine.

Just looking at that pine cone, I realize something important: it isn't sitting along the side of the road crying because it isn't good enough. Neither is the Milky Way galaxy. So why are we crying? Why are we struggling with insecurity, with the sense that we don't have strengths or that our quirks might just swallow them whole?

We can't miss the details. It's in the details that we find God still doing the spectacular work of creation.

When we look at our lives, full of the mundane in many ways, we must not miss the elegance of their design. We can't get lost in what we see as flaws when the fact that our hearts beat independently of anything we do makes us miracles. We can't look at our homes and see the chaos of Cheerios on the floor and shoes strewn not quite where they belong when these very details reveal the gift of life between our walls. When we feel insecure, we can choose to see God's intentional design in all of creation.

We can't miss the details. It's in the details that we find God still doing the spectacular work of creation that we may be tempted to think ended in the book of Genesis. Check it out right here, in another of David's psalms, where he proclaims,

> You changed my mourning into dancing . . .
> so that my whole being
> might sing praises to you and never stop.
> Lord, my God, I will give thanks to you forever.
> (Psalm 30:11-12)

Let's unlock part of this verse with a tool that Rick Warren calls the "Pronounce It" method of Bible study: we read a short passage of Scripture and accentuate one word at a time. As we emphasize each word, a different aspect of the passage's meaning pops into focus.

Being a learning nut (that's one of my favorite quirks about myself), I tried using that tool to reflect on this passage. I didn't get far before I was wowed with what God showed me:

"*You* changed . . ." It's God who makes this happen. Not us.

"You *changed* . . ." It's a done deal. In the past. The issue isn't getting it to happen but realizing that it has. My breath got caught in my throat when I emphasized this second word.

God *changes* our mourning into dancing. The verse doesn't say God *replaces* our mourning with dancing. It says God *changes* it; God takes something that seems unusable and redesigns it into something useful and even beautiful, important.

When God gets hold of our "mourning"—our intensely personal struggle over unanswered prayer, ongoing battles, or weaknesses—it actually *becomes* dancing. God can shift one part of ourselves or our lives—something tough or awful or frustrating—and morph it into something else altogether without scrapping the raw materials.

You've seen this in your life, I'm sure. Think of a situation or relationship for which you can't fathom a benefit, and you aren't sure you can hold on long enough to see it. Think of the choice you have to make that puts you way outside your comfort zone, so far outside you fear you'll lose your bearings about what you believe. Then, somehow, maybe in the middle of it—but probably well afterward—you see what God did. How God interrupted all possible trajectories of how that situation, relationship, or choice could turn out and made it better—made you better—than you ever imagined.

It happened for me as I went through infertility and longing for motherhood: the pouring out my heart, facedown on the bed, spent past anything I had to give in prayer. The uncomfortable treatments, the unsolicited advice from friends or even strangers, the waiting and hoping and sobbing. Without that season, I'd never—not in a million years—have been strong enough to handle the children I finally received from God. I simply wouldn't have had the emotional muscle or sheer stubbornness needed to advocate for their special needs, to dig in and help the older two heal from early emotional wounds of foster care.

God is the original recycler. When it comes to aspects of ourselves that we can't stand, that's not only encouraging, it's also a breath of fresh air for all of us more than seven billion people on planet Earth. While we are learning to better reduce use of, reuse, and recycle physical resources in our increasingly crowded world, we can trust our Designer to do that work with our personal, internal resources too. It's the three Rs of life. God reduces our anxiety as we trust in him. God reduces our insecurity as we learn more about who God made us, and we start to own our designer quirks. God reuses our strengths over time, building our understanding, wisdom, and endurance as we continue to engage people and situations. God recycles our quirks, refining and repurposing them into the strengths they were always meant to be.

What relief that God has made us and the situations we face completely recyclable! God doesn't waste anything in us or our lives. Not one thing. Will you believe that today, friend?

Knowing this, what can you say to yourself today when insecurity creeps up on you? Take a moment to write it here.

12

Your Wonderful and Why It Matters to the World

T HE WEIRDNESS-TO-WONDERFUL journey is part of how we answer the constant human question: *Why am I here?* Do you wake up every morning and know, deep down inside, the answer to this question? Not just what you *do* while you're here but also the underlying *why*? Without overthinking it, can you answer these questions quickly and clearly about yourself?

> What's unique and wonderful about me?
> Why does that matter to people in my life?
> How do I invest my talents daily?

There are many examples in history of people uniquely equipped for situations. Albert Einstein had a groundbreaking way of seeing math and physics and the tenacity to overcome failing math as a child to get there. Helen Keller possessed a stubbornness that kept her alive long enough to meet Anne Sullivan and then to persevere out of dark silence into language, relationship, and advocacy for those with blindness worldwide.

In the Bible, I've always liked the story of Esther. This young Hebrew girl, captured by the enemy, rose to become queen and saved her people from an evil plan. What's not to like about that? But even Esther didn't always know what she was about. She had natural gifts; she was gorgeous, articulate, and gracious. As with most of us, though, she needed a little time and thought to figure out what these talents would mean for her—and for God and her people. Let's see what her story reveals about the "Why am I here?" question and how strengths and quirks play into the answer in her life.

Many of us read her story one, two, twenty times and see only the story of a brave, beautiful girl turned rescuer of her people. But if we look a little deeper, can we see the struggle in her? The "Which way will it go?" question for each of her natural attributes? If we look deeply at those who seem to be perfect, we'll see even they arrive at moments when they must choose which way their quirks will lean: toward love or toward hurt.

Pastor Mark Driscoll of Mars Hill Church reminds us that Esther's story is more complex—and thereby more richly instructive to us—than we often give it credit for. It's not, he argues, simply the story of a good (read: unrelatable) girl. He draws our attention to the less obvious facets of her story, saying, "Many evangelicals have ignored [Esther's] sexual sin and godless behavior to make her into a Daniel-like figure, which is inaccurate."

What? Sexual sin? Godless behavior? This sweet girl, this Bible character, Esther? Perhaps Pastor Driscoll's words upset us as we read them. After all, Esther didn't struggle with quirks and weaknesses, right? She is an example to us.

Oh, but wait a minute. There was that part where she, as Driscoll points out, "[spent] around a year in the spa getting dolled up to lose her virginity with the pagan king like hundreds of other women."

Yes, even "perfect" young Esther suffered from her innate gifts dipping into the dark side. Her beauty and submissiveness—qualities that shone strongest when she risked her life to save her people—were presented as seductiveness and people-pleasing earlier in the story. This provides an example of how natural tendencies aren't good or bad in themselves, but they positively or negatively affect us and others depending on who's powering them.

> *Natural tendencies aren't good or bad in themselves, but they positively or negatively affect us and others depending on who's powering them.*

Perhaps you can relate to this. In earlier chapters, we've talked about how different traits can be strengths or weaknesses. Let's look more closely at how they shift from one to another. You'll notice in Esther's story that nothing is mentioned early on about her fasting, praying, or attempting to use her natural tendencies according to God's will. During that time, she lived her natural tendencies powered by her own ideas, energy, and thoughts. It's a combination we all consider pretty great, especially in the United States, and especially as women in the postfeminist era. We can do anything if we put our minds to it, right?

Esther's life says a big *No* to that.

Without God empowering her strengths, she was just another face in the king's harem. A pretty one, granted. She captured the king's heart more than the others. But her beauty wasn't going to last forever (the number of antiaging products available to us in drugstores attests to this!). In the right hands, however, it could leave a legacy beyond all she ever imagined. Later in her story, when Esther chooses to live from her natural tendencies, powered by contemplation and fasting (Esther 4:16), she brings about justice and saves her people from genocide. What a difference the power source makes!

Esther's characteristics—her weirdnesses, if you will—included traits like submissiveness, beauty, eloquence, and grace. In each situation her weirdness could reveal itself to be a strength or a weakness, depending on whether she leaned into self-serving or God-serving. The dark side or the life side. Her issue was never that she needed to become less like herself and more like someone else. Esther, like each of us, was made in God's image, reflecting certain aspects of who God is. In her case, the unique blend of quirks and qualities was the winning combo for her and her people. What might be the impact of your living your quirks in God's hands—in their life sides?

That's where the questions from the beginning of this chapter come into play. You probably already recognize the aspects of yourself that make you unique. I hope that as we've journeyed together through this book, you've begun to see ways those traits are wonderful. But what about the way they affect others? What might be possible in your family, community—maybe even the world—because of those tendencies? What could God do with your intense focus, your need for order, your ability to talk for hours, your way of finding the bright side when nobody else thinks there is one? How might people's lives change for the better in the presence of your stubborn insistence on excellence, your bigger-than-life dreams, or your empathy for people whom others may try to ignore?

When we not only see the value of our quirks but also open our hearts to dream a little about why they matter in the world, the gift God's given becomes tangible and truly magnificent.

Take a look at the three questions at the beginning of this chapter. How would you answer them today? If you had to make a guess about why you're here based on your quirks, what might that reason be?

13

Your Tools for Living Strengths with Confidence

QUESTIONS ARE SOME OF OUR MOST powerful tools. They turn the unknown into an opportunity and the challenging into a conversation. One of my favorite ways to get out of a rut—in relationships, work, spirituality, or any other aspect of life—is to ask questions. Brian Regan, a comedian I love to watch, jokes that it's the only real skill politicians have: the ability to ask questions, especially when trying to evade answering someone else's!

Politician or not, if we don't learn to ask good questions, we can miss out on the treasures in our quirks. Good questions open us to possibilities. They serve as tools to unearth the gifts in our quirks, to help us polish the strengths that are rare or hard to work with—traits that take creativity, or maybe a second opinion, to appreciate fully.

We have lots of tools available to us—here in this book, in our network of support, online, through classes and books. Questions are among our most important, but they're also sometimes hard to muster when insecurity, fear, or frustration arises regarding our quirks. Because of that, it's helpful to have a few good ones on hand to keep the strengths excavation moving along. In this case, our question-tools have one thing in common: getting back to the basics of who God designed us to be.

Here are questions to keep handy when wonder is in short supply:

What do you love to do? What activities energize you? What sparks your curiosity, your attention, your loyalty, or your longing? What could you do for hours at a stretch and not even notice time's passing? To what do you gravitate whenever you have a spare moment?

What are you really good at? What do you do well with little effort? What comes naturally to you? What are you known for, whether others appreciate it or tease you about it? What task makes you feel as though you got off easily when it's assigned to you in a group project?

What do you instinctively do first on your task list? You may not love doing this, but it's easy and straightforward, maybe even energizing for you. Why is that? What about that task makes it easy to tackle?

Whom do you most enjoy being with? What about them do you enjoy? What feelings do they bring out in you? What are they known for? How have they shaped your life or perspective?

During what part of the day are you most creative? Do you get up early to maximize that quiet, productive time before the rest of your household stirs? Do you get your best writing or projects done during the wee hours of the morning? Do you (like me) have a two-hours-before-lunch burst of energy and productivity?

Where do you most enjoy being? What is it about that space that meets a need, fills a gap, inspires, or energizes you? Is it the colors? The smells? The food? The sense of adventure? The restfulness?

The answers to these questions give us a clue about our strengths, which in turn can help us discover more areas in which to employ them.

I'll be the first to admit, however, that while these questions help us hone in on hidden strengths, they aren't always enough. We need a few more tools in our bag of discovery, especially when life happens and we're swept up in the busyness of the day to day. For those moments, perhaps it's time to grab on to this truth: when we can't discern the strengths in our quirks, or we're feeling discouraged that weaknesses are pulling us down, "the Spirit comes to help our weakness. We don't know what we should pray, but the Spirit himself pleads our case with unexpressed groans" (Romans 8:26).

The answers to these questions give us a clue about our strengths, which in turn can help us discover more areas in which to employ them.

This promise is one I lean on when dinner's on the stove, my kids are melting down in spectacular ways, and I'm looking at the clock, wondering how it isn't bedtime yet. I rely on it when I step into a new role in a suspected area of strength and I suddenly realize I'm in the middle of a much bigger pond than this little fish feels ready to navigate.

It's a promise for all the moments when we suspect God's beginning something great in us but all we see are our current circumstances, or when we wonder if God will ever do something great in us, considering the current circumstances.

While we're searching and trying to figure ourselves out, even if we have the best questions possible in our bag of tools, there's comfort in knowing that we have a helper along for the journey. That God's Spirit is present with us, helping us figure out what to ask, where to look, and how to respond gives us the courage to pick up our tool bag and keep living faithfully, one step at a time, in pursuit of living our weirdness wonderfully.

What would change in your life and activities if you started asking the right questions in the face of insecurity?

14

Your Known Strengths and Discovering New Ones

ONCE YOU BEGIN TO SEE the life sides of quirks that have seemed destined to drag you down, the door is wide open for wonder to flood in. Keep it open, and soak in that wonder with a few more questions and tips in mind.

First, consider what you love most. In the previous chapter, I mentioned that we can discover strengths asking, *What have I always loved to do?* A strength, by definition, is something you do really well, just about all the time, with little effort. This is why you can find them hiding in your favorite activities. It's energizing—fun, often—to do what you're great at. And it looks different for each person.

I discovered this after studying strengths for a little while. As I looked back over my life, even before I took any strengths inventories or read about the topic, I'd known since high school that I loved to encourage people, go on road trips, and study for tests. (I know, this last one probably sounds weird. But weird is what we're talking about in this book, right?)

As I entered college, got part-time jobs, and dated people, the best memories I have include these three things: encouraging, traveling, and studying. Those late-night talks encouraging roommates still make me smile. The year abroad, backpacking through a dozen countries on a shoestring budget, still creates an ache in me to get on the city bus and ride it someplace—anyplace—just to be around new places and people. In fact, I still ride the bus as often as I can just because I love it. And the studying? Well, I'm sitting here, researching and writing this book, aren't I? Yes, I still love to read, study, and learn new things, twenty years after high school.

What about you? Do you love talking to people? Organizing events, parties, or your house? Do you create intuitively—whether it's new formats for that expense report or a new recipe in your kitchen? Maybe you love to daydream, and you have fun thinking of a hundred ideas a day about life and the projects you're doing.

Whatever it is, write down what you love. Then read through the list and ask yourself, *What about my personality—how I engage and respond to the world—makes these activities so enjoyable?* That's the next step in strengths-discovery, friend. It's there that you better understand who God made when God made you.

Second, look for the strengths hiding in plain sight. Sometimes strengths are right in front of you, thinly disguised. But they'll show their faces if you keep searching for the *why* behind the things you love to do. For example, if you love to listen to people, talk to some others you know who also love listening. Brainstorm together what it is about listening that really fills your heart and life. Consider that part of what you love, paired with another thing you love to do. Are there any similarities? Anything the two activities or kinds of situations have in common?

A friend of mine loves to run. We met early on a Saturday for a run around a local lake. Spring had exploded vibrant blooms of color everywhere. I looked to see what she loved so much about running. Was it the gorgeous floral aroma? The warmth of the sun? The energy visible in runners, cyclists, and even kids on training bikes? The runner's high at mile four? I wanted to find out, so I asked her what she liked about it. But no luck, she was lost in music. Her favorite worship tunes pounded through earphones, putting her "in the zone," oblivious to everything else.

Once I got used to the thought that I wouldn't be encouraging anyone that morning, I turned to another of my loves: studying. And, yes, I just admitted to studying one of my best friends like a lab rat. I told you learning was one of my quirks.

As we ran, I thought more about what other things I knew she loved: good food, travel, singing. And there it was: she loves running because she loves music! And she loves music because she loves singing—which she's done in worship ensembles at different churches for just about her entire adult life.

What about you? What are your "I love X because I love [something that seems totally unrelated to X]" activities? They may seem unconnected to your strengths, but chances are, as with my friend, there is a connection somewhere if you look deep enough. And once you find it, chances are it will be a very life-giving piece to your "me" puzzle.

Third, find a mentor. Connect with people who are clearly doing what they love and are good at, even if it isn't the same talent you have. Just watching how others develop their purpose will give you lots of ideas for your journey. And having someone to encourage you when you hit bumps in the road is an invaluable asset.

If a mentor isn't available to support you in a certain strength, avail yourself of books on living your strengths, such as the ones by Marcus Buckingham or Women of Faith. Go online and watch YouTube and TED videos, noticing the speakers, presenters, and artists, because they will reveal, in words or responses, different facets of strengths you're wired with. Take notes. Keep a journal handy—paper, digital, or whatever works—so you can record all you're learning along the way.

Finally, try out those strengths. The best way to confirm that a strength is a strength is to start using it. This means two things: saying yes to more of the activities that employ your strengths and no to more of those that don't. It also means testing positive outlets for tendencies that are quirky or classically challenging for you.

By intentionally investing in more of what you naturally do well, you invite more enthusiasm, efficiency, and energy into your life.

By intentionally investing in more of what you naturally do well, you invite more enthusiasm, efficiency, and energy into your life. Doing this creates an upward spiral. And it opens the door for God to work in you in ways that are "abundantly [beyond] all that we ask or think, according to the power at work within us" (Ephesians 3:20 ESV).

Keep practicing those strengths, even if it's awkward at first. And trust me, it will be. Especially as you start testing positive uses for your quirkier tendencies. It's a little stiff and stilted, just like learning to walk, read, or ride a bike was at first. Keep looking for ways to use those talents anyway. Keep exposing yourself to the strength. You'll be amazed at how intricately, beautifully, and well made those strengths have always been in you. Even the weird ones!

Your turn! Become a strengths detective. For the next few days, notice what roles you love, which tasks give you energy, and what efforts bring positive responses from others. Write them down. Use this chapter to help explore them.

15

YOUR LIFE'S WONDERFUL STORY

A S WE DISCUSSED EARLIER, everything about you has something to do with your purpose: The music you love. The things that freak you out. Your favorite hobbies. Your job. What you think about. The classes you took during college. The summer job that had nothing to do with anything (or so you thought). And even that weirdo you dated in high school.

It all has a point!

If you're like me, you might be thinking, *Yeah, right! How exactly could all those parts of my life be related? And how could they possibly matter to real life now?*

I asked myself that question one night years ago as I stared at my new, empty blog. I wondered, *Why did I start this anyway?* Everything was in pieces around me (literally—my house had flooded a few months earlier). My youngest, just a year old, was having unexplained seizures. We had just adopted our two foster daughters that summer, and something was clearly amiss with the older one. The mental health diagnoses wouldn't become clear until later, but regardless, I wasn't sure we could go through with the adoption. In fact, I didn't think I could go through much more, period.

That season seemed to be another random, disconnected part of my life to stash away—I hoped deep down and far away!—in a box in my mental cellar. Right along with my penchant for eating rock salt from the sidewalk when I was a preschooler. Or hiding a stray kitten in my room during junior high. Or struggling through my parents' divorce.

At that point I did something really hard. In response to an assignment from a class I was taking, I drew up a time line of my life, looking at the past for where God's presence had been and ahead for where God might be leading.

I considered three questions during this assignment:

- What words might appropriately describe my life over time?
- What experiences have I had, and what have I gained from them?
- What ideas and experiences inspire me?

After I had done this, I stepped back mentally to catch the panorama of the "forest through the trees." To my surprise, words and themes were repeated again and again: *coach, teacher, inspirer, supporter.* In my role as the oldest sibling growing up. As a teacher's assistant in middle school. As swim team captain in high school. As swim coach afterward, and then as a resident advisor in charge of helping college freshmen find their fit on campus. As a middle school teacher. After that, as an AVID (Advancement Via Individual Determination) teacher and coach with struggling students (the role that probably best prepared me to adopt foster kids). Even the photography studio job had a place in my bigger purpose, as I had helped create settings that reflected and supported each subject's uniqueness.

My whole life, it became clear, had been one huge becoming. It all mattered. Every single part. Just as every part matters in yours.

My whole life, it became clear, had been one huge becoming. It all mattered. Every single part.

Just as every part matters in yours.

And what of the tough season during which I was starting my blog? It gave me the passion to help others get through challenges and grief—to get unstuck and enjoy their lives with renewed confidence—even in a season when I was struggling to find that myself.

You may relate to my life of ups and downs or not. But you have a story full of events that sometimes seem random and disconnected—impossible to fit into some sense of purpose or unified theme. You think there might be one in there somewhere, deep down and hard to reach, but right now you can't see it.

May I encourage you in this journey of pressing into your purpose? Don't get distracted by the jumbled-up mess you see on the surface. Trust that God knows what he's doing. And ask God to share with you the view of your life and purpose from his vantage point. To give you a glimpse of the artistic design—the special part of God's overall design defined as you—which brings unique beauty to the world.

Consider the three questions I asked myself. What answers emerge based on your life so far? From the direction in which you seem to be moving? Where is God in your story?

PART IV

DIGGING DEEPER INTO YOUR WONDERFUL

You can find energizing moments in each aspect of your life, but to do so you must learn how to catch them . . . and allow yourself to follow where they lead.
—Marcus Buckingham

MY OLDEST DAUGHTER is a treasure hunter. No matter what we are doing, she trains eyes on the ground as we walk from place to place, searching for treasure. Never mind that we live in a city where she's more likely to find trash and old cigarette butts than something worth keeping. Don't try to tell her that anything of value will already have been picked up by someone else. And definitely don't tell her to throw away trash/treasures when she picks them up unless you want an earful or possibly to have something thrown at you.

I have no idea why she is so adamant about finding treasure. But I do know that it's reminded me of something crucial: you won't find treasure in life unless you look for it.

It's a truth underscored by an incredible story that happened in 2009 in Staffordshire County, England. Terry Herbert, a metal detectorist, asked the owner of a local field if he might sweep the property to find treasure. The field's owner, Fred Johnson, allowed Terry to do this, even though his farm had been swept by detectors before and nothing was found.

Terry swept the property deliberately, patiently. He wasn't looking for anything in particular, but he knew from experience that there's treasure all around. He expected to find something good, whatever that looked like.

And, boy, did he ever!

Two hundred forty bags of ancient Anglo-Saxon gold and silver artifacts worth £3.285 million (close to $5 million US) were lying, long undisturbed, under this neighbor's farm. It became known as the

Staffordshire Hoard. The two men split evenly the value of the find, and it changed their lives forever.

If Terry had never asked, "What might be under that field I pass every day?"—even after others had asked, tried, and given up—he'd have missed his treasure. If he hadn't kept an open mind about what his find might mean, he might not have approached the British authorities to validate the value of his discovery. If Terry's detector had indicated a find but he hadn't dug to find out what was below that field, we all might have missed out on the gift his simple act gave to our knowledge of history.

We've got to get curious, get moving, and get digging in order to find the treasures in ourselves.

When it comes to our quirks, we'd do well to think like Terry. We've got to get curious, get moving, and get digging in order to find the treasures in ourselves. We've got to stay open to whatever treasure we find—even the rare or hard-to-work-with traits that take creativity or maybe a second opinion to appreciate fully.

Those Staffordshire men's lives will never be the same, simply because of a decision to search for treasure on land a farmer had owned for years without imagining its value. We can live our entire lives with unknown treasure—gifts, strengths, quirks—buried in ourselves too. In this section, let's unearth that treasure together: first, by examining the best model we have for living weirdness wonderfully and, next, by gathering powerful tools to make the dig productive.

16

Following the Leader Toward Wonderful

WHEN IT COMES TO LOOKING for treasure, we've already seen that some of the most precious material is what God wove in to who we are. That we were created in God's image, assembled in the womb to reflect a unique combination of divine traits. We're all chips off the Old Block, children designed by God to be like God.

What do children like to do? Emulate everything! They dress up like mom and dad, talk like us, walk like us, put on makeup like us, argue like us, connect with others like us, study like us. At least when they're little, before the do-the-opposite-of-mom-and-dad teen genes kick in.

Each of my kids reflects characteristics or abilities of my husband and me—it's how people know we're family. God designed us to be like that with him too. We're encouraged to "imitate God like dearly loved children" and to live our lives "with love, following the example of Christ, who loved us and gave himself for us" (Ephesians 5:1-2).

As my kids learned to talk by mimicking me, we're to learn how to use our strengths and quirks by mimicking our earthly example of God's heart: Jesus. The Bible says Jesus was fully God and fully man, so our Savior struggled with quirks just as we do. Jesus wasn't some feet-never-touch-the-ground mystic. Jesus was a weirdo, and Jesus was wonderful. A quirky person but a perfect (complete) one. All the time. In every interaction.

> *Jesus wasn't some feet-never-touch-the-ground mystic. Jesus was a weirdo, and Jesus was wonderful.*

Jesus was tempted in *every single way* we are. Jesus was tempted in his pride, courage, security, planning, giving, preferences, and personality. Jesus had all the same potential weaknesses we do, and with each choice he faced, Jesus revealed the strength instead of the weakness in his quirks.

In the pages of Scripture and the accounts of Jesus' life, we find the guidebook for how to live weirdness wonderfully if only we take the time to see it. We can trust Jesus understands our struggles as we take a look at some of the possible quirks Jesus revealed and how he handled them.

Weirdness #1: Jesus seemed irrationally bossy. Jesus talked with unexpected authority that incensed contemporary religious and political leaders. Jesus gave his disciples difficult and sometimes impossible instructions. Here's one example: "Late in the day, his disciples came to him and said, 'This is an isolated place, and it's already late in the day. Send [these more than five thousand people] away so that they can go to the surrounding countryside and villages and buy something to eat for themselves.' He replied, 'You give them something to eat'" (Mark 6:35-37).

If I'd been there, I would have reacted exactly like Jesus' followers (and here, I'm paraphrasing): "Me? Give them something to eat? From what, the rocks and dirt? You're nuts!"

But Jesus managed seeming bossiness and irrationality in a life-giving way. Jesus broke through what the disciples thought possible and opened doors for people to see God's miraculous power as never before. The Son of God's "bossiness" brought greatness to lives and circumstances because he always employed it to give glory to God. Five thousand contented bellies and twelve basketfuls of leftovers later, bossy looked pretty fabulous.

Weirdness #2: Jesus seemed unfocused. Jesus frequently stopped midjourney to heal people, be with kids, and say things that seemed irrelevant or even inappropriate to those traveling with him. In one instance, while traveling through Jericho to the next area of ministry, Jesus stopped, looked up in a tree, and made lunch plans with the tax collector who'd climbed up to get a better look at him (see Luke 19:1-6).

But Jesus' seeming attention deficit disorder had a life side: availability wrapped in love for people. Jesus always emphasized that the Son was on earth to be about his Father's business (Luke 2:49). And as John 3:16 states, that business has always been to love the world so much, so deeply, that God would give his own Son so we could have eternal life. Jesus lived and died loving others, even when it interrupted what others regarded as his daily agenda or what they felt were the highest priorities. In fact, Jesus lived this quirk so well, he modeled for us—more than two thousand years later—the cure for what author Richard Swenson calls the "vertigo" of having a life so overplanned that we can't focus on or handle anything well!

It may seem bold of me to suggest that Jesus was quirky, but if we're honest and we don't overspiritualize his humanity, we can't deny that fact. If we do, we miss something huge about Jesus: "We don't have a high priest who can't sympathize with our weaknesses but instead one who was tempted in every way that we are, except without sin" (Hebrews 4:15). It's because Jesus was tempted in all the same ways we are that we can lean into the same power Jesus did and therefore live in the life side of our nature just as Jesus did.

That power Jesus leaned on: Is it really sufficient to guide us past temptation to act on the dark sides of our quirks? Can Jesus really have known how hard it would be for us in these complex times? Yes. How do I know? Because the power Jesus held onto is the power that raised him from the dead (Ephesians 1:20). Call me nuts, but I'm going to guess that trumps whatever power our quirks—even the most intense ones—may seem to have over us today.

Is it hard to picture Jesus with quirks? What hope does the idea that Jesus struggled with quirks give you in your journey?

17

Living Wonder When
You'd Rather Not

YOU PROBABLY ALREADY KNOW this, but the best way
to transform your family into psychos is to try to get them to
church on time.

And if you're like us, raising kids, the last five minutes before
departure for church is the perfect time for one of them to spill an
entire glass of milk on herself, deny it, and require United Nations–level
negotiating skills to get her out of her beloved wet jeans and into much
less cool ones. Come to think of it, that we arrived only twenty minutes
late that day is pretty awesome.

But I didn't think so then. As we pulled up to the church and
unloaded the first three kids, only to discover this one had snuck her wet
jeans back on while we drove, and had gotten milk all over the backseat in
the process, it took everything I had not to become the Hulk and punch
in my car door. Being a good Christian mom (ahem), I coaxed her from
the car, dragged her to the ladies' room, and attempted a smile for the
greeter, whose eyes widened as she beheld the child with the sweatshirt
tied around her head sulking behind me.

Not the perfect morning. Or was it?

After closing the door to the restroom, pushing back tears and frustration, I began to see it.

Shame.

All over her face. And her heart. And if I were honest, all over mine too. Because her mess and sin revealed mine. Hers was outward at that moment, while mine was hidden. She sometimes disobeys or gets controlling when she's overwhelmed. I smile when I'm angry. What's the difference, really? It's all the dark side of our weirdness. For her: the dark side of being resourceful. For me: the dark side of being an encourager and leader, even when I'm not able to be either to others in a given moment.

That realization gave me courage to let my heart speak louder than my judgment and frustration right then. I knelt down on the bathroom floor, unwrapped her face from the sweatshirt she hid behind, held tear-stained cheeks in both hands, and said the words that shatter shame: "I love you."

The words that pour light into a dark place. That bring back to a moment the real reason we're all here anyway. Because while I want my kids to be honest and take care of our things (and you can be sure she had to clean up that mess later!), the most important commandment is, Jesus said, "You must love the Lord your God with all your heart, with all your being, with all your mind, and with all your strength. The second is this, You will love your neighbor as yourself. No other commandment is greater than these" (Mark 12:30-31).

From that moment with my daughter, I found some tools we all can use to let love in when our dark sides take over:

- See what's behind the broken. Notice what's underneath the frustrating behavior or response. It's not easy. So ask the One who sees behind the sweatshirt—God will give you eyes to see who he sees in there. He will bring images and words and encouragements to mind that will shine light on the life sides of their strengths and give you the strength to help them lean into those.

- Stand for what's best for the other person. Become her champion and biggest fan. Encourage her with words that point out the good you know is in her, even if she's not choosing it then. Pray for her to know how valued she is. Pray out loud in the middle of the public bathroom if you have to. Stand for the truth, for the promises in God's Word that come to mind as you support her. Fight in prayer for what is best for this person.

- Celebrate that she let the sweatshirt fall away. That she lets you love her. Celebrate that she's growing and trying, that she matters to God. Celebrate the moments when God brought someone like that for your ugly dark-side moments, and even when God gave you the courage to get through them on your own. It's so easy to get caught up in the tough moments—to leap from one urgent issue to the next—that we sometimes have to deliberately choose to celebrate. Don't skip this part. You need it, and so does that person you are loving toward her best.

We all have those funky moments, those reactions and responses that send us into the dark sides of our weirdness and make life uncomfortable for others. Just as when the men stood poised with stones ready to crush the shame of the woman caught in adultery, God presents us with a challenge: "Whoever hasn't sinned should throw the first stone" (John 8:7).

We're all weirdos in our own ways. Will we become judges of the weirdness around us? Or will we let love keep us not only from our own dark sides but also from needing to define others by theirs too? It's in life's bathrooms, right smack in the mess of life, that we have the opportunity to let love live in us. We have an opportunity to let love move weirdness—ours and theirs—toward wonderful.

Perhaps a particular situation or relationship came to mind as you read this story. What's one way you might let love shape your weirdness in that circumstance?

18

LEARNING FROM SOME OF HISTORY'S BEST-KNOWN WEIRDOS

Learn from the mistakes of others. You can't live long enough to make them all yourself.
—*Eleanor Roosevelt*

JUST AS WE LOOKED AT JESUS' seeming quirks and how he handled them well, we can learn from others in history who put their weirdness to good use. Let's look at a couple who did that and at one who didn't manage quite as well.

Although he may or may not have been a vampire slayer, Abraham Lincoln most certainly was a quirky guy. Tall, gangly, with unruly hair, this Kentucky son of what scholar Michael Burlingame calls "unremarkable" parents had the wit to match any upper-class child of his day. Probably more. Known for his wit, eloquence, intellect, and spirituality, Lincoln still had qualities with dark sides, just as we do. His cousin Sophie said, "The worst trouble with Abe was when people was talking—if they said something that wasn't right Abe would up and tell them so. Uncle Tom [Lincoln's father] had a hard time to break him of this."

This bluntness quirk showed up in Lincoln's boyhood and continued throughout his life. It apparently drove his dad crazy, but it wasn't an intrinsically negative trait. As an adult, Lincoln found the perfect use for it in politics. In a world where others talked for hours without saying much (not unlike today!), Lincoln's tendency to be blunt led to one of the best-known American speeches of all time: the ten-sentence masterpiece we know as the Gettysburg Address. Middle schoolers across the United States still breathe a sigh of relief at the brevity of this oft-assigned text for memorization.

Thomas Alva Edison, the famous inventor of the electric lightbulb, was an influencer and tinkerer. Born the youngest of seven to a family of little money, suffering from partial deafness, Edison showed great creativity in getting people on board with his ideas, even as a child. In his book *The Wizard of Menlo Park: How Thomas Alva Edison Invented the Modern World*, Randall E. Stross shares a series of telling stories about this talent, describing the young inventor as "precocious," a "boy tycoon," and a "wheeler-dealer." His likability and influence with peers allowed him to work harder than most without antagonizing people, in such a manner that he easily secured investors' trust and funding for projects, even early in his career.

Edison also had a knack for innovation. His father was a lover of politics, but Edison preferred taking things apart and concocting improvements for tools and machines. The combination of his influence and innovation gifts opened the door for him to become one of the first nonpolitical and nonmilitary celebrities in the United States. We're talking superstar status! Like any superstar, Edison had quirks with potential dark sides. They appeared in the ease with which he embellished stories for greater public impact and the creative ways he pranked friends and colleagues—using, yes, you guessed it: electricity. Throughout his life and interactions with the public, Edison had a choice to make: lean into the catalyzing strength of his innovations and influence or squander it on mischief and overblown celebrity. For the most part, he did more of the first, leading to his development of the phonograph, lightbulb, and other inventions we still depend on today.

Another innovator, Clara Barton, was driven by empathy, determination, and an intense sense of responsibility for the care of others. Anyone who has been a caregiver for any length of time knows how easily those strengths devolve into their dark sides of martyrdom, codependency, and poor self-care. Clara suffered from all these quirks privately and intermittently during her career while bravely caring for Civil War soldiers and later developing the American branch of the International Red Cross.

In order to be an unmarried woman on the front lines of battle at a time when women didn't do that, Clara had to use her fierce determination. She also faced an internal battle with perfectionism and a sense that she needed to portray herself as different from who she was. This dark side of Clara's empathy—this oversensitivity and unfounded belief that the public and even her young female students wouldn't respect her—led Clara to push people away and isolate herself from close relationships. She "bore dreadful shocks of exposure, and faced hideous scenes, with equanimity and always with unflinching valor" but lived emotionally alone because she never fully mastered the dark sides of her empathy and responsibility strengths. They didn't keep her from doing spectacular things for people and the world, but her weaknesses certainly decreased her quality of life and sense of worth, just as they can

Any strength can become a weakness when overused or used in a context that hurts us or others.

do for us when we allow the dark sides of our quirks to go unchecked.

These well-known people reveal aspects of the truth that any quirk can be a weakness, just as any strength can become a weakness when overused or used in a context that hurts us or others. May we take Eleanor Roosevelt's advice and learn from these and others—in what works and what doesn't—so that we can lean more fully into the wonder with which we're wired.

Can you relate to any of these famous individuals? If not, who in the public eye have you noticed with quirks or gifts like yours? What might you gain from their experiences?

19

LETTING CRITICISM
STRENGTHEN YOUR QUIRKS

HOW DO YOU HANDLE CRITICISM? Is it the aspect you dread in relationships? Does it leave you feeling hurt, offended, or inadequate?

When we pour our hearts, words, creativity, or effort into something—whether at work, in ministry, in writing, in parenting, or in friendship—it's easy to get defensive when someone criticizes us. But what if we were to change the way we thought about it? What if we began to accept criticism not as an affront but as an opportunity?

Trust me, I know it isn't easy! Criticism and I have a long, sordid history. Raised the oldest child in a single-parent home, I needed to feel like I was OK, which to me meant feeling confident and competent. I would hide mistakes and sometimes even lie about circumstances and choices in order to escape criticism. As an adult, I still have to make the constant mental choice not to hear criticism as rejection or judgment.

A while ago, two people I love and respect confronted me with critiques about a particular issue. It was something that mattered to me—and that I really could have messed up if I'd continued down that path. As they shared their viewpoints, the dark side of my high-achieving "do it well" quirk started to wrap around my throat and choke the joy right out of me. Childhood insecurities wanted to tie the criticism to my worth and value as a person, as though what I do could ever replace who I am. By the middle of the conversation, I wanted to run away and hide.

Criticism, whether welcomed or not, can open our eyes to bigger wonder than we may know is possible for our quirks.

We all get there sometimes with feedback, especially on topics dear to our hearts, don't we? With such clamor in my mind in that moment, I didn't recognize the value in the critique just then. Instead I was upset, hurt, offended. But shortly afterward I realized how God wanted to use the unsolicited evaluations to move me in a better direction—one I'd otherwise have missed. It was a moment when I started not only to know the words of King Solomon but also to absorb this freeing reality: "Without guidance, a people will fall, / but there is victory with many counselors" (Proverbs 11:14).

Experiencing victory and overcoming challenges come in many forms when we're faced with criticism. Criticism, whether welcomed or not, can open our eyes to bigger wonder than we may know is possible for our quirks. What opportunities—gifts, even—can lie in the seemingly negative observations of others? Here are a few that come to mind.

Criticism helps us discover more about ourselves. Our response gives us a clue about what matters to us, how deeply we believe in what we're doing, and how confident we are as people. It also helps us better understand the other person. What she shares and how she shares her opinions offer clues to what she likes, wants, and finds valuable.

Criticism provides a trigger to choose the life side rather than the dark side of our weirdness. Our first instinct is to feel threatened. But what if we allowed criticism to hang there in the air, without defending ourselves, long enough to truly see it and come away with more wisdom and understanding about ourselves? What if we let it show us what we're good at and what areas still need work?

Criticism opens the opportunity to grow toward something better. Many times constructive criticism from a trusted source has saved me from taking an action I would have regretted. I'm grateful for those timely directional signals and for those thoughtful individuals who had the courage to be honest with me! They've helped me remember to spend time looking, listening for, and seeking the best possible choices. With all we're doing, it's easy to miss the wisdom that comes from pauses evoked by solid critique.

Criticism cultivates a healthy sense of who we are and what we can do. In other words, it develops our humility muscles. As we learn to lean into that healthy personal honesty, we discover a greater sense of appreciation and fulfillment in our lives, work, and relationships.

Criticism provides material to build relational bridges. Responding graciously to feedback opens the door for deeper relationship with those we love and respect. After all, how far can you go with others if they're never able to disagree with you or tell it as they see it?

Criticism lets us know when a relationship is unhealthy. If the other person constantly criticizes, it may be time to set healthy boundaries, take a break, or accept the gift that relationship was for a season, and move on.

It's easy to recoil when someone makes a critical remark, well intentioned or otherwise. It's much harder to face it head-on and find the jewel that lies within. But if we take the gift of feedback and let it create growth, build relationships, keep us realistic, and help us make better choices, we'll discover the process is honing our quirks into the gems they're meant to be. And as a bonus, it reveals that people notice what we're doing and care enough to see us do it well.

A year after the situation I just mentioned, the people who offered that critique are still a daily, important part of my life. They're even more significant now than they were before the confrontation. Beyond that, having looked closely at their feedback—and my intense reaction to it—I rediscovered that criticism won't kill me, and it can help me be more intentional about choosing the life side of my achiever quirk.

Whether criticism seems to be a gift in the moment or not, there truly is a benefit waiting in it for you. Are you willing to let that wonder-building blessing into your life today?

When has a well-placed bit of criticism helped you grow person-ally? How might you further welcome criticism into your weird-ness-to-wonder journey?

20

Riding the Sleep Train
to Wonderful

S ET DOWN THAT THIRD CUP of coffee and take a moment to
answer this: Are you getting enough sleep?

Anyone who knows me knows that I would qualify as
president of the Sleep Is Overrated Club. A trip to the East Coast for a
conference recently threw a monkey wrench into my outlook on this.
When I got back home on the West Coast, I was tired three hours earlier
than usual, so I went to bed—but slept until my usual waking time.
Suddenly, after eight years of life as a mom (and a decade prior to that as
an overachiever), I was getting eight to nine hours of sleep a night.

The earth didn't cease to rotate. My kids still ate decent meals. My
house looked the same. And I lost no ground in terms of writing or
productivity. I actually started getting more done than before the trip.

How could this be? I wondered.

As I did a little research about sleep, to see whether this was just a
fluke or it needed to become my new normal, here's what I discovered.

You're less *you* without adequate sleep. We all know the negatives to
sleeping less than we ought to: brain fog, low immunity, more wrinkles,
less patience, more mistakes, worse moods. You could list ten more

without much thought, I'm sure. But here's the real kicker: when we don't get enough sleep, all those cumulative negative effects limit who we are—our strengths, dreams, vision, and impact in our families, work, and ministry. Inadequate sleep leaves us shadows of who we could be and makes the battle to live the life sides of our quirks almost impossible to win.

Sleep fuels happy brains. And happy brains allow weirdness to become wonderful.

Sleep fuels happy brains. And happy brains allow weirdness to become wonderful. Adequate sleep helps us think clearly. Brain fog is real, and having the right amount of sleep reduces that neurological effect so we can focus on our lives and goals. We enjoy better moods when we have enough cycles of light sleep, which come after the deeper, REM dreaming at the beginning of sleep (that is, after the initial five hours on which too many of us survive). A better mood leads to a more positive life outlook, which in turn gives our dreams and quirks a fighting chance.

Enough sleep also boosts our creativity. As we pursue life dreams and press into living our weirdness well, we'll face challenges. Creativity makes those challenges more like speed bumps than roadblocks as our minds work more efficiently through problems at a subconscious level.

If you're not getting enough sleep:

- Don't stress out. Getting anxious about not sleeping enough will make it hard to sleep when you have the opportunity. Listen to your body. When you're tired tonight after the kids go to sleep, take a good hard look at what you need to get done for home and work, and do the top two things. Then go to bed.
- Limit light before bedtime. Artificial light tricks our bodies into thinking it's still daytime, which makes it easy not to listen to their cues.

- Take naps. Set a timer for 15 to 20 minutes and let yourself rest before you tackle—or continue tackling—the chores, bills, or to-do list.
- Stay away from caffeine late in the afternoon or evening. Everyone's body is different, so work with this one. For me, caffeine after 3:30 p.m. means I'm up all night.

There are a thousand and one ways people recommend getting more and improved sleep, but ultimately it's about doing what helps you live your life fully in your strengths—so you can make a difference in the world around you. Why not make that process a little easier by giving your mind and body the rest they need?

If you struggle with getting enough sleep, consider keeping track of your sleep habits. What do you notice? What changes might you need to make so you can give those quirks a fighting chance at greatness?

PART V

Handling Weaknesses
and Waywardness

Be sure that the ins and outs of your individuality are no mystery to
[God]; and one day they will no longer be a mystery to you.
—C. S. Lewis, The Problem of Pain

LOOKING AT THE X-RAY AS A fifteen-year-old, I wondered if the technician had snapped an image of me dancing rather than lying still on the steel table. "It's scoliosis," she said. This, I discovered, is code for the fact that my back curves in the wrong places and makes me look weird in fitted clothes (unless you think it's cool to have one hip noticeably higher than the other).

My scoliosis looks weird, but it's not in and of itself a bad thing. It all depends on what I do with it. If I don't keep my muscles strong, scoliosis becomes a real pain in the neck. And back. And hips. When I do take care of it, my crooked, weird-looking back is actually a gift. It motivates me to stay healthy and strong. To stay fit and not let myself go as I age. My skeletal weirdness keeps me intentional about my health.

You have scoliosis too. Maybe not physically in your back. But your unique tendencies and innate gifts are like my scoliosis. They make you different, weird even. They're not empirically bad. They're not even weaknesses in and of themselves; they're simply reality.

What matters is how we manage our scoliosis—our quirks—as well as our weaknesses and mistakes along the way.

This section delves into the differences between our uniquely quirky gifts and the weaknesses we all share. It digs into these essential questions: Will we let our quirks get out of shape and make our lives and others' lives painful? Or will we keep them strong and let them be the gifts they can be?

21

THE DIFFERENCES BETWEEN
WEIRDNESS AND WEAKNESSES

WE OFTEN THINK OF WEAKNESSES and quirks as interchangeable, yet in reality they're very different. Quirks are what make us unique. For the purpose of this book, they're our weirdness, our design, what sets us apart and becomes our fingerprint on history. They're made up of our God-given talents and the spiritual gifts and personality tendencies that color how we display those talents. Because of this, there is only one you-version of weirdness. Nobody has the same types or proportions of natural strengths, spiritual gifts, and personality traits you have. You're your own special mix of quirks and talents, desires and callings, roles and responsibilities.

Unlike our highly unique weirdness, weaknesses are common to all of us, and they come in many forms. The first type of weakness is a lack of ability resulting from our neurological development. As we grow from infancy onward, our brains create pathways—neural connections based on how we think and respond to the world. The strongest nerve connections and pathways in our brains form the traits in us that are most prevalent and can become our personal strengths. The weakest neurological connections eventually are abandoned so our minds can focus on the strongest ones.

Author and life coach Holley Gerth boils down this process in her book *You're Already Amazing*. There she affirms that God has given each of us certain clear strengths and that part of the way God accomplishes this is by strategically wiring us with certain weaknesses too. She explains, "Our divinely created strengths (fueled by God's power) are actually supported by our weaknesses, because if we were good at everything, we wouldn't focus on much of anything." These ability-weaknesses give us permission to live fully in what we're best at. And they open possibilities in relationship with others because our weaknesses mean we need each other. It's a gift—and challenge—we'll talk about in chapters that follow.

> *Our ability-weaknesses shape us by making us who we aren't, as much as our strengths and quirks make us who we are.*

Our ability-weaknesses shape us by making us who we aren't, as much as our strengths and quirks make us who we *are*. They'll never be as prominent as our strengths—as much as we sometimes wish we could naturally do things we can't—because we literally aren't wired for them. That's not to say, as Holley writes in her book, that we should let them cause problems for us. If roles at home or work require certain abilities, and some aren't areas of natural strength, we still need to find ways to handle that, either by partnering with someone who's skilled where we're not or by finding other solutions.

Shannon Cassidy, strengths coach and executive director of Bridge Between, Inc., offers an unconventional but effective workaround for these kinds of weaknesses. When we identify skills required for roles we love (or sometimes simply have to fill), and we can't delegate to someone with natural ability in that area, we can try something most of us would balk at: "Just stop doing the activity we loathe and see if anyone notices."

Before you pass out—especially our sweet perfectionists—Shannon goes on to explain why this makes sense: "Some tasks originated as great ideas or processes at one time and may have been replaced. They may no longer serve a purpose." For me, a childhood tomboy turned mother of four girls, this idea is a breath of fresh air! It took approximately one hour of motherhood to realize I was lacking the neurological pathways for fancy hairstyling. Oh, I tried to make up for this deficit, believe me. But the feather-headed, squirmy, post-foster-care (read: grieving, don't-you-dare-try-to-get-a-brush-through-my-hair) toddlers in my house had no interest in my developing this weakness into something more.

Freedom came the day I let go of my inferior cosmetology complex, went to the store, and purchased detangler and a decent brush. The kids still don't have fancy, praiseworthy hairdos for school pictures, but they're sufficiently groomed not to garner negative attention. And with that weakness happily set aside, I have put more energy into what I *am* skilled at: talking through strategies for the playground drama that happens regardless of hair status at school.

A silly example, certainly, but evidence nonetheless that our ability-weaknesses are purposeful. They support us in being fully who God intended us to be by giving us permission to specialize in what we do best.

This viewpoint may be hard for some of us, especially in the Christian community, who've come to believe it's godlier to shun our natural giftings as an act of sacrifice because embracing them is prideful. I recently watched a video of author J. I. Packer sharing his impression of why we need weakness. The video is a montage of images, revealing how it's much harder for the aging Packer to do what used to come naturally. The video's final images show how, even with the limitations the author now faces, God still does amazing things with Packer's writing. The video concludes with this statement: "Weakness is the way."

As I looked at those closing words, I both agreed with and agonized over them. While it's true, as Paul writes, that we must learn to "boast" about our weaknesses (2 Corinthians 12:9 NIV), that doesn't mean we should intentionally try to live in them. To be God-loving people doesn't mean we must find every possible way to do what we stink at, to serve in ways we hate, or to work at tasks that make us want to run and hide.

To favor our weaknesses above our talents just so we can say God's strength is perfected in them employs the same faulty logic that Paul rebuked when believers in Rome espoused choosing to break rules in order to elicit more of God's forgiving grace (Romans 6:1-12). It dishonors God's image when we deliberately act on what we're not good at for the sake of some twisted notion of humility. Humility is honesty. And the honest truth is that each of us is gifted at certain things. Humility is being who we are—being good at certain things, all the while admitting that, like a flashlight devoid of batteries, our gifts can't shine without God's power.

So don't fall for the lie that investing in your strengths prevents God's strength from filling your life. Instead, ask God what he imagined when he designed you. When you stop asking this, a different type of weakness shows up: the struggle between selfishness and love.

What's one thing you're unable to naturally do well? How has that inability—that weakness—allowed you to develop your strengths?

22

THE INVISIBLE BATTLE BEHIND
YOUR WEIRDNESS

ONE OF MY FAVORITE BOOKS to read to kids is Bill Martin Jr. and Eric Carle's *Brown Bear, Brown Bear, What Do You See?* Sitting on a carpet, wide-eyed preschoolers listen, guessing the next page's animal. Each page turn and drawn-out "What do *you* see?" elicit big "I see a blue horse [or whatever's on that page] looking at me!" answers from the children.

Over a lifetime, our seeing shifts from noticing what's in front of us to evaluating what it means before we even see the whole picture. Physically, age gets the better of us. But more than that, the eyes of our hearts can get cloudy—blurred by stress, expectations, and obligations. Hindered by fear, worry, and grief. Blinded by anger, frustration, and loneliness. We often lose sight of the goals we once had and our immense value. (And isn't it interesting that we phrase it that way—to lose sight?)

But it's what we can't see that most obstructs our vision of the wonder that God designed in us. Author John Eldredge says, "The reason you doubt there could be a glory to your life is because that glory has been the object of a long and brutal war."

In his book *Waking the Dead*, Eldredge implores us to see the context in which we're living—to see the spiritual behind the day-to-day tangible. He writes, "War is not just one among many themes in the Bible. It is *the* backdrop for the whole Story, the context for everything else. God is at war. He is trampling out the vineyards where the grapes of wrath are stored. And what is he fighting for? Our freedom and restoration."

John then shares one of the most game-changing ideas I've ever seen in a book: "Until we come to terms with *war* as the context of our days we will not understand life. We will misinterpret 90 percent of what is happening around us and to us."

Think about that for a minute. Can you see it? Hear it? The spiritual bullets flying around you 24/7? The booming bombs? The people charging, running, wounded? The victories? The defeats? Wave after wave after wave of battle, and we're right there in the middle of it all, living in our whole mess of laundry, errands, relationships, and desires.

Is it any wonder, then, that we have trouble seeing? With all that smoke and gunfire, we'd need some pretty powerful eyewear to see at all. Paul knew that back in his day, too, as he shared this prayer—one that's still for us today: "I pray that the eyes of your heart will have enough light to see what is the hope of God's call, what is the richness of God's glorious inheritance among believers, and what is the overwhelming greatness of God's power that is working among us believers" (Ephesians 1:18-19).

Without the eyes of our hearts—the intuitive, Spirit-led vision God gives us as his kids—we live blind. We miss the point. And without this kind of vision, we're tossed back and forth by the additional human weakness the Apostle Paul described in his letter to the Romans: "When I want to do what is good, evil is right there with me. . . . It wages a war against the law of my mind and takes me prisoner with the law of sin that is in my body" (Romans 7:21, 23).

This kind of weakness—our internal drive to prioritize what we want above the needs of others or the wisdom of God, paired with moments we fall prey to the spiritual battle around us—limits God's power in us and prevents the abundant life we desire. It hinders that abundance as we contract universe-sized possibility to what we think we know and want.

You know the moments I'm talking about, right? They always happen when we intend to be or do something meaningful in our callings or relationships. For me, it's the days when I need to speak, write, or otherwise think clearly. Days like today, when my feet barely touched the floor next to my bed before World War III broke loose among my kids. When the

> *In that moment we have a choice: fall prey to the battle—to our weaknesses and the weaknesses of people we love—or choose something better.*

toilet plugged ("Who thought it would be fun to flush a tea cup?"), I threw on my hybrid-between-jammies-and-workout clothes (the ones we moms mean to change after breakfast but then realize the next morning we're still wearing). It took sophisticated negotiations to get my arguing, grumpy kids through breakfast, and by 10:00 a.m. I had to banish them to the four corners of my house so there'd even *be* a house for my husband to return to after work. Who can think, plan, or use any of her strengths and quirks well in that onslaught?

If we took a minute to evaluate ourselves in those high-intensity moments, we'd probably find we're breathing shallowly, our shoulders are tense, our vision has shrunk from big picture to what's urgent right now. We move into survival mode. In that moment we have a choice: fall prey to the battle—to our weaknesses and the weaknesses of people we love—or choose something better.

What, exactly, is that better thing? Jesus said,

Don't worry and say, "What are we going to eat?" or "What are we going to drink?" or "What are we going to wear?" Gentiles long for all these things. Your heavenly Father knows that you need them. Instead, desire first and foremost God's kingdom and God's righteousness, and all these things will be given to you as well. (Matthew 6:31-33)

In this principle we find a powerful tool to prevent our strengths from becoming our biggest weaknesses. When we trust God to provide our every need on this battlefield of life, we can turn our energy to doing that job unique to us—living our weirdness wonderfully.

How would your vision of yourself or your situations today change if you saw it in context of the epic invisible war around us?

23

The Way to Keep Worry from Weakening Your Strengths

A S I SAT DURING ONE OF THOSE MOMENTS I mentioned in the last chapter, trying to think of the next passage I needed to write for this book, the clouds gathered. Dark, tumbling, intimidating thoughts—worries about whether the message would come out clearly or get lost in a million tangents.

Automatically, I did what I often do when I start freaking out and letting my quirks become a weakness: put the energy toward something else, something more productive. I opened the devotional app on my phone, and there they were—the words that have been dear friends and guides to me for twenty-three years, since I first discovered God's love and redemption. They've walked me through high school, college, big choices, dating, marriage, births, deaths, and everything else in the past two decades: "He will keep your ways straight" (Proverbs 3:6).

In a new moment when worry started to cloud my hope, these familiar words snapped me out of what could have become a hurricane of negative emotions.

Raise your hand if worry is one of the quirks you'd love to send packing! I know, I hear it all the time with friends, family, clients. But contrary to what we may think, the natural bent toward mulling over ideas itself isn't good or bad; it's just a feature of how our minds work. What you do with that energy when it comes up will determine whether you worry yourself into a hole or walk yourself into God's presence and purpose for you. The key to doing the latter is to spend the energy on something else. Following are some ideas.

Become a detective. Think Sherlock Holmes if you have to. Whatever you do, make it your job, your passion, to find evidence of where and how God is leading you as you navigate what's got you worried. The Bible promises that seeking good, seeking God, will always be rewarded: "When you search for me, yes, search for me with all your heart, you will find me" (Jeremiah 29:13).

Point your worry at God. Pray about the situation you're facing and the people involved. Pray for people you know who are struggling or worrying about issues of their own today. Pick up a newspaper and pray about situations that worry people across the globe. Prayer is worry with feet. Use it! Trust the encouragement that God promises: "The prayer of a righteous person is powerful and effective" (James 5:16 NIV).

Bring the worry into the light of day. Say it out loud to a friend, a neighbor, or even your cat. Getting a worry out of your head and into audible words puts the fear right in front of you, which causes a shift: either you realize how unrealistic the worry is, or you hear it in a fresh way so you can take a next step to solve the problem.

Read Truth to your worry. When the worry comes up, read Scripture. Start with Ephesians to get a good handle on your position in Christ. Worry really, really hates that. It would much rather boss you around, bind you in fear. But Truth reveals worry for the sad weakling it is and gives you fuel to move forward in hope. This is why the people who wrote the Psalms spent so much time considering God's words. They knew those words mattered more than any they'd ever pen and often implored

God, "Let my cry reach you, LORD; / help me understand according to what you've said" (Psalm 119:169).

Write a letter. Thank a friend or family member for a time he or she encouraged you. Feel the paper in your hands. Watch the words come from the pen. Walk it to the mailbox and breathe the fresh air. Again, doing this gets us out of our heads. And as a bonus, it takes all that worried energy and puts it to good use as we live wisdom like this: "So continue encouraging each other and building each other up, just like you are doing already" (1 Thessalonians 5:11).

Learn something new. Read up on the issue you're worried about. Talk with knowledgeable people to find out how they handled it. Keep all that info in a journal or file so it's accessible when you need it, and when you finish studying, walk away and leave the issue and its worries there in that journal. Don't worry (ahem). It will be there when you get back.

By practicing that last step, I discovered something about worry: it's normal. As King Solomon wisely said toward the end of his life: "There's nothing new under the sun" (Ecclesiastes 1:9). Not our weirdness. Not our wonder. Not our worries. When we let that sink in, worry begins to dissolve. After all, how worried can we really be about something if we realize we're one in a line of countless others in history who have faced whatever's got us shaking in our boots? People have worried about work since immediately after original sin in the garden of Eden (Genesis 3:17). Parents have worried about their kids since day one, and for good reason: Adam and Eve's kid, Cain, was the original problem child (Genesis 4:8).

Worry happens. But it's not new, nor is it a crisis. It's simply another feature of who we are—a response that, like fear, can cause us to determine whether a situation needs to change or whether we need to change in some way. In my example of trying to write this book, worry helped me see it was time to pull in some resources to help me with the logistics. With four young children at home and a book to write, I'd bitten off more than I could chew, and worry helped me see that. But I didn't dwell on the worry. Instead, I chose to pray about my worry ("God, I'm freaking out here. Help!"), search for ways out (getting help at home, letting go of other projects for a time), and speak Scripture out loud—words such as "Don't worry. . . . Your heavenly Father knows that you need [time, money, whatever]" (Matthew 6:31-32). Honestly, I'm grateful for worry's help as I put this book together. It opened a door for strategic thinking and possibilities I might not have considered otherwise.

Worry became a tool for me to live my strengths, and it can be the same for you. When you notice it beginning to swell inside, turn and look it in the eye. It's not nearly as scary as it would have you believe. When you choose not to let worry boss you around, it may give you just the burst of insight or energy you need to follow God's lead into your wonderful.

What are your favorite things to worry about? How might you redistribute that energy toward more life-giving thoughts and actions?

24

THE WAY TO PREVENT QUIRKS
FROM BECOMING WEAKNESSES

I MENTIONED EARLIER THAT MY significance strength once broke me down in tears in a staff meeting. But that wasn't the most spectacular meltdown that quirk has caused in my life. The first memory I have of this weirdness was back in eighth grade when I, a relatively new transfer to that school and peer group, ran for student body president. Seems normal enough, right?

With a platform of "Let's get better cafeteria food!" I'd made posters with before-and-after drawings: green hamburger caricatures on the left side, fresher, multicolored ones on the right. "Vote for Laurie! Sign the fresher food petition! Get food you can actually swallow for lunch!" the posters read. Or at least they would have read that, if not for the profanity and, ironically, the cafeteria food smeared across the words.

What kid who wasn't in the popular, designer-clothes-wearing crowd would run for a middle school government position? And why would anyone vote for the little-known girl with esoteric notions of revamping the cafeteria when any normal eighth grader just wanted more school dances and ice cream served on Fridays?

Most people could see where I erred in this process. But not me. I was out to change the entire district's food services program. (Because a thirteen-year-old getting three hundred signatures from kids at her school can do that in real life, right?)

It was on speech day that my grandiosity came crashing down around me. Or to be more precise, the pencils and lunch items students threw on stage came crashing down around me. Because while I was thinking big and pushing the envelope, I smacked into the truth of Shannon Cassidy's words: "Any strength overdone is a weakness." In my case this meant I stood face-to-face with four hundred annoyed-looking reminders of the wisdom that people don't care how much you know until they know how much you care. I didn't care about the students, I cared about the issue. I cared about bringing big fat change that wasn't even possible for me at that age.

Fortunately, as a new believer in God at that same time, I had someone to go to for comfort when my strengths came back to bite me: the Apostle Paul. His weakness was related to his strength too. He had some sort of issue that was a struggle for a long time, one he pleaded with God to remove from his life (2 Corinthians 12:7-9). Many of us can relate to doing that with our own "thorns," our quirks. What exactly was his thorn? One possibility offered by many scholars is poor vision—an interesting problem for someone with such great spiritual vision, right? Whatever the physical issue Paul's thorn represented, another challenge he had was the same one we all face with our strengths and quirks: the battle for who's in charge.

Prior to Paul's becoming an apostle and missionary of the early church, he'd been trained as a teacher and leader in the Jewish temple (Philippians 3:4-6). His strengths in learning, leading, and passionate belief led him to persecute and kill Christians before he met his match on the road to Damascus, as recounted in Acts 9. It was only when Paul gave God true authority over his strengths and quirks—when he turned them toward investing in and loving people—that these gifts began to change the world.

As a kid who'd just been run off a political stage, I found hope in

Paul's story. If this guy who'd used his zealous quirks to kill the opposition could find life-giving, loving ways to use those gifts, anyone could. The key to making the shift seemed to be given here:

If I speak in tongues of human beings and of angels but I don't have love, I'm a clanging gong or a clashing cymbal. If I have the gift of prophecy and I know all the mysteries and everything else, and if I have such complete faith that I can move mountains but I don't have love, I'm nothing. If I give away everything that I have and hand over my own body to feel good about what I've done but I don't have love, I receive no benefit whatsoever. (1 Corinthians 13:1-3)

It was only when Paul gave God true authority over his strengths and quirks—when he turned them toward investing in and loving people— that these gifts began to change the world.

Paul knew from experience that any strength could be a weakness. His passion. My significance. Esther's beauty. Mary DeMuth's deep thinking. Your quirks. Your neighbor's. We find in Paul's story that the key to a tendency being a strength is our ability to love others. Since God is love, the Bible tells us we can love others when we know God and have encountered his love in us (1 John 4:19). As we spend time learning about God's heart for us in Scripture and lean into those truths, we find both the love and the ability to love that make our weirdness wonderful.

When did your strengths or quirks come out in unloving ways? How might you invite God to redeem that incident or relationship with his love?

PART VI

BOUNCING BACK
FROM WONDER BUSTERS

Do the next right thing.
—*Max Lucado,* You'll Get Through This

S HE SHIFTS IN HER SEAT AND LOOKS uncomfortable. She almost always does. Her words convey insecurity, grief, and loneliness. It doesn't matter how many friends she has, what kinds of clothes she wears, or which neighborhood she lives in. She's aching inside, and she just keeps on aching, month after month, year after year.

I've been that woman more often than I want to admit. You've probably been her too. Many years ago, someone like us sat next to a hot spring on a daily basis. Paralyzed, he was unable on his own to get to the water, where rumor promised healing. For years he sat, frustrated, discouraged, seeking more and not knowing how to find it. Then a stranger walked up to him and asked, "Do you want to get well?" (John 5:6).

What a stupid question, the disabled man must have thought. Or maybe it was more like, *Duh! Are you kidding me?*

But the questioner wasn't asking whether the man wanted to walk again; there could be little doubt he did. He was asking something far more fundamental. The original language of this passage phrases it more like, "Do you intend to become [exist] whole and complete?"

Do you—will you—intend . . . ?

Will we choose life? Will we decide we'll live whole and full despite whatever lack or challenge we face? The man who was paralyzed needed to want it. We need to want it too. We need to choose it and keep right on choosing and wanting and hoping for better no matter what happens or how tough things get.

This section shares five common wonder busters and how to choose to get back on track when they arise.

25

USING MISTAKES TO SHIFT
WEIRD INTO WONDERFUL

I'M A FAIR-WEATHER FAN of running. There's a reason for this, beyond the fact that I have a love-hate relationship with running in general: where I live, we get so little rain that on the rare occasions it falls, the first drops cause our whole city to forget how to drive and to whine incessantly about the fact that we don't own umbrellas as we stand, soggy, in supermarket checkout lines.

Worse than the dreary local attitudes on rainy days, the mere change of routine brought by something like rain can lead to pretty silly mistakes. One day, when I chose to go running with my daughter and dog, it looked as though the rain had stopped—not that I would know how to confirm this, as a resident in a city of rain amateurs.

For this particular running adventure, I picked my favorite place: a nearby lake. It's inspiring, refreshing, and the perfect distance around. The dog and I often ran there while my daughter rode her bike twenty yards ahead, taunting me like a drill sergeant to pick up the pace. Prior to this one fateful day, I thought the only negative about running there was the gnats. Turns out that wasn't the case. But I did learn a few things:

1. Dogs don't respond well to having rain dumped upon them.
2. Or to being bombarded with half-inch hailstones.
3. Or to running around a lake with no shelter when #1 or #2 occurs.
4. And neither do eight-year-old daughters on bikes.

Oops!

Whether you've made a blunder like this or not, you've most certainly made a mistake or two in life. We all do. Some are minor and irritating. Others are devastating to us or those we love. In the midst of those debacles, how will we handle them?

First, face them. Take responsibility for whatever you've done. Otherwise one mistake multiplies into two. It's hard to own up to what we do, especially when we struggle with insecurity and guilt. But when we take responsibility for our choices and actions, we demonstrate wisdom and open the door to opportunities to reconnect with whomever we've adversely affected. Because we more quickly make things right, we don't waste time floundering in denial. And even better, our honesty helps us avoid making the same mistakes again later on.

Second, learn from them. Mistakes are great teachers. Many brilliant people staunchly assert that we learn more from our mistakes than from our successes! Think about your more recent flubs, gaffes, misjudgments, or bloopers. What might they be trying to teach you? How can you grow in light of that knowledge? What will you do differently next time? Be careful here to avoid thoughts that seem like learning but really represent shutting down to people and opportunities—resolutions like "I'll never trust anyone again."

Third, recognize the value of experience. A lot of mistakes occur in the process of trying something new or experimenting with a fresh approach to a familiar issue. Be courageous and decide you're going to relish the experience of learning from your mistakes. Even if the outcome at the time was truly painful or even catastrophic, there are probably precious jewels of experience you've gained through the experience. As a friend recently pointed out, "Erasing [all our mistakes] would just leave a blank space—that's not very interesting." So treasure the results of your errors. And give yourself a little credit for trudging through the work it took to find the bright spot. This process contributes to making you who you are: a unique, beautiful creation God loves with all his Father heart.

We can spend a lifetime stewing over mistakes, beating ourselves up, or we can cut ourselves some slack.

Fourth, move on. We can spend a lifetime stewing over mistakes, beating ourselves up, or we can cut ourselves some slack, apologize to those we've hurt, make amends, and move along. There's nothing to gain from wallowing in our missteps except a loss of forward motion. And fearing our next mistake can paralyze us. As Elbert Hubbard put it, "The greatest mistake you can make in life is to be continually fearing you will make one." Decide to walk through the mistakes. To learn from your goofs. To absorb the experience and move on.

As we learn from mistakes, we do something our adversary (see chapter 22) doesn't expect from us: we symbolically take back control from him and put it in God's hands. Once there, our mistakes transform from the blight we thought they were to the polish that makes our weirdness more wonderful.

⌘

What's a lesson you've learned from one of your recent mistakes?

26

RELEASING PERFECTIONISM'S
GRIP ON YOUR QUIRKS

A S WE DISCOVER AND GROW IN OUR unique strengths, quirks, and life purpose, the roadblock we'll often hit (especially we women) is the loaded, loathed idea of perfection. When I asked fans of my Facebook page, "What do you think of when you hear the word *perfect*?" they responded: "Unreachable." "Impossible." "Anxiety-inducing." "A burden."

As a mom, I've responded through the years by doing what any seasoned perfectionist would do: try hard. I parented just as the best parenting books suggested. I said the right things. Looked to the right specialists. Spent more quality time with my children. When one of my girls needed far more than even this well-trained perfectionist could give her and I had to let her go for that time away from home (see chapter 3), it jolted me from this routine. First, because it revealed that no matter how well I parented her, my worst perfectionist fears were confirmed: I actually wasn't enough—my daughter needed a whole team of professionals to help her. And second, because it revealed how broken I'd become in the hands of perfectionism as her mom.

That year showed me just how insidious perfectionism could be and how much it could erode our natural gifts. When I sat in my daughter's counselor's office and had to make tough decisions about her treatment, my natural talents of brainstorming and boldness faced perfectionist questions that challenged my confidence in who God designed me to be. This stemming from the fact that perfectionism's one talent is to make us question ourselves: what we do, how we relate, the ways we learn and grow and invest in life around us.

In the situation with my daughter, I heard questions like these: *Will this treatment help her heal? Will it negate the work we've done with her so far? Will it show her we love her? Will it push her away?* But more than anything, perfectionism interrogated me: *Laurie, will you make the right choice? Will you do it right?*

Maybe you've been there too—not necessarily on a couch deciding your child's next therapeutic move, but deciding something else altogether, something unique to your situation. A move you need to make at work. A change in an investment. A decision about the care of an aging parent. A relationship that needs a shift in direction. A change in how you see yourself.

We all struggle with some aspect of perfectionism and tend to reason our way through it. We read books, attend seminars, and seek counsel. We struggle, get overwhelmed, feel inadequate, and lose sight of who God uniquely, beautifully designed us to be. But what if the issue isn't doing it right?

What if, when we read something like the familiar translation of Matthew 5:48—"Be perfect, just as your Father in heaven is perfect" (NKJV)—we internalize the text's true meaning? A meaning, as we discussed in chapter 1, that has nothing to do with flawlessness and everything to do with the fullness and completeness that the Greek word *teleios*, translated "perfect," conveys: "Therefore, just as your heavenly Father is complete in showing love to everyone, so also you must be complete."

If this is what God means by "perfect," then it's time to make peace with perfect, friend. First, because God is perfect. If there's no darkness in him (1 John 1:5), perfect can't be a negative, hurtful thing. Beyond that, God's law—God's instruction for humanity—is perfect (Psalm 19:7). That was bad news for humankind for a long time, since there was no way we could keep that set of rules on our own. But then God's perfect—complete, full—love filled in our gaps as Christ stepped in to take the

Although we'll never fully take hold during this lifetime of who God designed us to be that doesn't mean we're insufficient.

consequences that humanity deserved, giving us the freedom to interact with God without fear (1 John 4:18). That work Christ did on the cross was perfect too. It was finished, complete, permanent—an irrevocable gift for believers (John 19:30; Romans 6:10).

Perfect is a great word if you ask me!

Although we'll never fully take hold during this lifetime of who God designed us to be (Philippians 3:12), that doesn't mean we're insufficient. It means we need to shift away from clawing for perfectionism and instead focus on growing in confidence.

Just as our quirks and strengths are two sides of the same coin, so are perfectionism and confidence. Perfectionism is the dark side of confidence. It's what perfect becomes when we filter it through what other people think, expect, or seem to compare us to.

Confidence is knowing what you're here for, what you're good at, and what God wants you to do with the whole package. It's recognizing and taking care of that aspect of your life.

When we relentlessly focus inward instead of on God's design, we end up with a murky view of all we don't have and can't do. If we make it our life's work not to be perfectionists but to be confident in what God has made us to do and who God has made us to be, we'll find a life-giving new vantage point.

That is, I believe, what Jesus meant about taking on the light burden and the easy yoke offered to each of us (Matthew 11:30). We can begin this burden exchange from perfectionism to confidence wherever we are, regardless of how long perfectionism's been bossing us around. It starts when we agree with God.

Affirm what God is affirming in you. Confidence is all about agreeing with what God says is true. Perfectionism, in contrast, is agreeing with and pursuing everyone else's (including your) expectations.

As I bounce back from years of waning confidence and ballooning perfectionism, I need to make this choice habitually. I don't want to feel like a stranger to normal as a parent or as a woman. I don't want to feel like a failure or as though my mind is a tyrant. So I must choose daily to pursue true, honest, life-giving confidence.

Whatever I choose, however, the point is this: as a believer, perfect—complete and whole—is my default. It's your default too. And it's a dream-filling, confidence-building gift from the only One in the universe who truly understands the concept.

If we struggle with perfection, our struggle should not be to become the world's sad version of it, but to wrap tightly in the arms of a perfect God who leads us through life fully as he intends.

The next time your inner critic gets mean and starts to portray Perfect as a tyrant, tell it to take a hike. Perfect is your heritage, not your heartache. It's your identity in Christ, not an impossibility.

What could life look like if you chose to see yourself in confidence rather than through the murky lens of perfectionism? Will you take that risk today?

27

OVERCOMING FEARS
TO LIVE QUIRKS WELL

Courage is being scared to death—and saddling up anyway.
—John Wayne

LIFE SCARES THE HECK OUT OF ME SOMETIMES. Most of the time, if I'm really honest. When it comes to making the tough decisions, holding the line with our kids, being honest in relationships, fear can start to make me feel like a downright coward.

I'm not the only one in this boat. When I asked readers what one trait they'd change about themselves if they could, Jackie answered, "Being fearful of failure and the judgment of others . . . to the point that it has limited new things I have tried or experiences I have had."

Perhaps you can relate. If so, there's good news for you: even a scared-stiff coward can be brave because courage isn't a feeling. It's what you *do*, not how you feel. When you're doing the scary, step-out-of-your-comfort-zone things that chip away at your confidence, courage is active.

The Bible has a lot to say about courage. Through most of the Old Testament, two Hebrew words are used: *amats* and *chazaq*. In the original language, *chazaq* means "to strengthen, prevail, become strong, be firm, be resolute." In the New Testament, we find a comparable Greek word like *stēkō* (to stand firm) used dozens of times. The point is this: it's a process. Having courage in who we are—quirks and all—is a choosing. A doing. A living. Feelings have nothing to do with it!

Courage is also a gift, not something we have to muster. It's not something we conjure or strive for. It's something God creates in us. While you're doing brave things despite your fear, the feelings of bravery are building in you. Throughout Scripture, when God tells someone to "be strong and courageous," the original Hebrew words connote God's strengthening that person as God speaks (Deuteronomy 31:7, Joshua 1:7 NIV). It's an act of creation, just as at the start of time but ongoing in us every day. And it's already ours for the asking.

When we're trying to live courageously, we need a lot of encouragement! And guess what? The root words for "courage" and "encourage" are the same. In the New Testament we find the term *parakaleō*, which means "to advocate, to comfort, to come alongside and strengthen" (encourage).

Here's the kicker: the name of the Spirit of God, who is given to all who believe, is *paraklētos*, a form of the verb "to encourage." This means we have powerful, life-giving encouragement every moment, every day, in every situation. We are, truly, not alone.

Courage transforms fear into a tool. When we step out in courage, we discover what's worth that risk and what isn't.

Knowing these things helps us let courage transform fear into a tool. When we step out in courage, we discover what's worth that risk and what isn't, all the while honing our sense of discernment. Jackie explains how acting carefully has helped her: "There have been times, like in a really big area of my life—employment—where I have been extra cautious and made very thought-out decisions that have benefited me and my family beyond belief." And beyond benefits in courageous caution, Jackie has seen God use fear to propel her into prayer for people and situations that a more naturally courageous person might miss.

More than anything, courage comes from choosing to love. What would it look like in life's scary situations if we decided to fall back on (or into) love for God and others? What if it wasn't about the scary situation at all but instead about loving well? Paul said, "If I have the gift of prophecy and I know all the mysteries and everything else, and if I have such complete faith that I can move mountains but I don't have love, I'm nothing" (1 Corinthians 13:2).

When we grasp the fullness of this truth—that without love, we have nothing—the goal shifts from self-preservation and loss management to a drive to know love and the One who embodies it completely.

Going back to the moment in the counselor's office from the last chapter, as I considered how to best love my daughter, rather than how perfectly we could pursue treatment for her, something shifted. The wrestling settled. The peace pressed in. With the help of God's encouraging Spirit, I was able to press through fear and instead live my quirky need to achieve in a way that focused on loving my daughter completely. And I could think through all the options for her with courage instead of letting my thoughts drag me into worry.

Isn't it encouraging to know not only that we can choose to live our quirks well in the face of fear but also that we don't have to do it alone? We have the one true Encourager right there to help us all along the way.

What scares you? What are some practical ways you might apply the truth that love casts out fear (1 John 4:18)?

28

CHANGING YOUR RULES
TO LET WONDER IN

WE ALL MAKE UP SEEMINGLY arbitrary rules in life. If you sit and think about it for a minute, you'll realize just how many you've made. What side of the bed you sleep on. The time of day you stop for coffee. The colors you wear together. Those rare free-time activities in which you indulge. The ways you respond to people when they do certain things. The way you think about yourself when you look in the mirror.

A rule is a regulation (conscious or unconscious) that governs a situation or behavior. It's something we do or think by habit, but it is still at some level a choice. What kinds of rules do you live by? Do any of the following sound familiar?

- When I weigh X, I'm unattractive.
- When my kids are misbehaving in public, I'm a bad parent.
- When I'm hungry, I snack on chips.
- When something changes, I worry.
- When I'm tired in the evening, I surf the Net or watch a movie.

- When I pray for a certain length of time each day, God will bless me.
- When someone yells at me, I yell back.
- When someone cuts me off on the freeway, I get mad.
- When I say no to that request, I'm not being a good friend.

If you're like me, you probably don't think of them exactly like that. Do people really believe, *When my kids are misbehaving in public, I'm a bad parent*? As someone who's spoken to countless women's groups— and sat at the park or at lunch with friends even more than that—I know from experience that's how many American women think, even if we can't verbalize it in such a clear-cut way. We derive these internal messages from what we think others want, from what we've come to believe is acceptable, and from what the media conveys in news, ads, and television shows.

What would happen if we decided to change the rules that make us feel angry, frustrated, lonely, guilty, ugly, or stressed? What if we let ourselves reconnect with our childlike roots and challenge the unsettling thoughts, feelings, or responses that emerge in us with my oldest daughter's two favorite comebacks: "Is that really *fair*?" and "Is that really *right*?" As much as it bugs me when she questions every rule I make with those two retorts, I have to give her credit for doing what the Apostle John encourages us to do when we face messages, internal or external: "Don't believe every spirit. Test the spirits to see if they are from God" (1 John 4:1).

To test those spirits, we first have to notice them. So think of a recent moment when you got frustrated, upset, or sad. How were you feeling before that situation set you off? What happened next? How did that change the way you felt or responded? Holding that moment in mind, if you had to explain how your feelings got from point A to point B, what statement—what rule—might sum it up? Don't judge yourself for what you come up with, even if thinking it seems embarrassing or silly. We can't grow stronger, healthier, and more into the life side of our quirks if we don't get honest about where we are now.

What would happen if we decided to change the rules that make us feel angry, frustrated, lonely, guilty, ugly, or stressed?

Look at that rule, that thought. Is it fair? Is it right? If not, maybe it's time for different rules. Some rules that love you and others and God with all you've got.

What if the new rules were these?

- When I'm healthy, well groomed, and tastefully dressed (as in, my clothes fit my body and body type), I'm attractive. The scale doesn't matter.
- When my kids misbehave, I calmly redirect them or we leave the store.
- When someone yells at me, I walk away.
- When someone cuts me off on the road, I thank God for keeping me safe.
- When I say no to something, I'm helping myself to sustain healthy relationships.
- When I'm hungry, I snack on healthy foods.
- When I'm worried, I take a deep breath and take a break or go for a walk.
- When I visit someone who's difficult for me, I remember Scripture verses that strengthen my heart.
- When I'm tired, I go to sleep.
- When changes happen, I trust myself—with God's help!—to get through them.

We all have rules. They're part of every aspect of our lives, and they can either support the wonderful in our weirdness or make us weaker. The choice is ours.

What are some of your unhelpful rules? How might you adjust (or even replace) them so they can support wonder in your life?

29

DISCOVERING WONDER IN . . . DISCIPLINE?

JOYFUL ENERGY FILLED THE ROOM. Smiles were wide, eyes bright, hugs abundant. The aromas of cinnamon, coffee, and freshly baked muffins mixed with the sweet smell of swaddled infants. It was the first day of a new year of MOPS (an international group that provides community for moms of young kids). And what a celebration it was!

Until we read the theme verse for the year: "God didn't give us a spirit that is timid but one that is powerful, loving, and self-controlled" (2 Timothy 1:7).

Cue sound of tires screeching to a halt. Instantly our eyes glazed over. *Self-control*: the word that brings connotations of restriction, deprivation, rules, guilt, and boredom. If we exercise self-control, doesn't it mean we never get to eat the yummy stuff? Or spend three hours reading a good book (especially if there are dishes to do and laundry to fold)? Or watch our favorite TV show? Or even take a nap when there's a spare moment in the day?

Even worse, *self-control* conjures guilt as we compare ourselves to others who seem to be naturals at this trait. Like the woman sitting next to us with the two-month-old infant, the woman who gets up every day to run at 5:00 a.m. and makes the Proverbs 31 wife and mom look like a slob. We're already giving so much in our lives as women, wives, and moms. What value lies in cultivating self-control on top of it all?

How about courage and power instead of fear? "God has not given us a spirit of fear, but of power" (2 Timothy 1:7 NKJV). In the original language the word for "power" could most accurately be translated "inherent strength." You have—right now, as we've been discussing— unique gifts and strengths that make you especially equipped for your life, relationships, and challenges. Your strengths don't look like those of the person next to you, so stop studying her to find out what you're supposed to be doing in your life! When you have the self-control to choose to step into your role, it's like Cinderella wearing the glass slipper—it fits perfectly.

You see, when we know who we are and who designed us and assigned our complementary gifts and strengths, fear melts away and courage replaces it. As courage grows, so does the impact of who we are in the world around us—an impact that only we can have because it's born from the strengths and quirks that are unique to us. And as courage grows, so does our sense of power and energy to do more of what we're uniquely made to do. Especially in a world where it's so easy to compare ourselves to others, it takes a lot of power to shift into what God's calling us to be and do individually.

Beyond power, how about greater love instead of distraction? When we're looking at everyone around us to find out what we're supposed to do and how to live well, there's no room left to truly see the people we love—to spend time, undistracted and fully invested, focusing on who they are and the relationships we have with them. When we discipline ourselves to live within our strengths instead of focusing on those of others, life becomes fully, brilliantly ours instead of seeming like some black-and-white replica of the real thing.

Finally, how about peace instead of chaos? You know that moment when we're rushing to get ready for work, our toddler's tugging at our leg, our husband wants to know the plan for dinner and date night later in the week, the nine-year-old needs us to check that last homework problem, and we feel like an A-bomb that's just about to incinerate a square mile around us?

That's the power of self-control. It's about strategic living.

What if we'd finished the homework the night before as part of the routine? What if we'd gotten up when the alarm first rang instead of hitting the snooze three times (which would have been facilitated by getting to bed an hour earlier the night before)? What if we were to set aside one day every quarter to evaluate our family's activities and commitments—to be strategic in how we spend our time so we don't live life as a blur?

That's the power of self-control. It's about strategic living. About building our values into our lives, right down to the little things, and letting those values inform the demonstration of our strengths and quirks. It isn't about cutting out everything we enjoy. Or getting up at the crack of dawn to run four miles every day (unless that happens to be your thing). It's about fully taking hold of who you are and what your family values are and building around that so fear, distraction, and chaos aren't life's defining characteristics.

How might you embrace self-control in one small way, starting today, so you can discover more abundance in living your quirks and strengths?

PART VII

LEARNING FROM REAL-LIFE
WEIRDNESS AND WONDER

*The only path to amazing runs directly
through not-yet-amazing.*
—Seth Godin

H E PICKED AN INDIE BAND on his Pandora music app, and then turned to take in the miles of desert stretching east from the highway we were driving. With only his son and one of my four kids in the backseat, my brother and I enjoyed luxurious grown-up talk for the eight-hour drive home from our parents' house. He, an entrepreneur with a heart to encourage and build the team at his tech start-up. I, an admiring older sister who wonders when this man emerged from my little brother.

The whole way over, he'd coached me on how to grow my business and upgrade my website. For this second leg of the journey he turned to me and joked, "My turn!"

We both laughed, and then he launched into this: "You know my top strengths [he's great at planning strategy, casting vision for the business, and mentoring his team]. Why do I struggle so much with being indecisive? It's like I can't make decisions because I get stuck thinking about how choosing one route would affect another. I get so worried I'm going to make the wrong decision for everyone. It's like mental constipation!"

I skipped an obvious bodily function joke that beckoned and instead started asking questions to find out more about this weirdness he saw in himself. "What are some examples of where this happens most often? Is it worse at work, or is it consistent in your personal life too? Do you ever see benefits from this tendency? Does anyone else see it as a benefit, even if only in certain situations?"

With a bag of our favorite chips, we munched our way through all these questions and more. Hours later, we'd laughed more than solved problems. My brother had new leads on assets in his quirks, and I noticed some common thematic struggles with strengths had begun to crystallize.

Although infinite combinations of strengths, quirks, temperaments, and spiritual gifts exist, we seem to have only a handful of hang-ups with who we are as people. This section shares a few of the biggies, with examples from friends, family, colleagues, and readers who have honestly admitted the traits they wish they could change and courageously joined me in the journey to see their weirdness in a new light.

30

WHEN YOUR QUIRKS DON'T PLAY NICELY TOGETHER

NOT ALL BLESSINGS IN OUR lives complement one another all the time. We get that promotion and our house—another gift—bursts a pipe and floods the whole downstairs. Our children make us laugh, except when they're making us cry from the arguing in the car on the way to school. You get the picture.

It's true for the gifts in our lives, and it's true for our quirks. My brother's lament in the section's introduction reveals it well: he's gifted at strategizing, visioning, and caring for people under his leadership, gifts that sometimes don't play nicely together. It reminds me of how E. B. White lamented that he wakes up every day wanting to both change the world and have a great time, which "makes planning the day difficult." My brother may not be balancing these same desires, but he is trying to negotiate the life-giving sides of an intense thinking strength and a powerful social/emotional one. Considering that cognition and emotion get processed in completely different areas of our brains, is it any wonder he's feeling mentally stuck?

We all get that: a tug of war between our strengths and/or our quirks. In me, sometimes it's the fight between wanting to make a difference and wanting to get things done. One is big picture; the other is logistical and impatient with the first. Which one wins? And is there a better (or best) quirk to go with in any given situation?

Let's look at this issue through an example my friend Shannon shared with me. She explained that if she could change one thing about herself, it would be her frustration when she's trying to communicate her thoughts and ideas to people. She says she has a hard time expressing herself, and then "that makes me more insecure about how [others] will respond or what they'll think of me."

What may seem to be common insecurity reveals an important truth about quirks when we look a little deeper; sometimes they need to take turns.

You see, if I may brag a little on my friend, Shannon is one of the most gracious people I know. Having roomed with her our last year of college, I was up close and personal with her and this struggle she explained. Her strengths include creating harmony in relationships, affirming others, solving problems, and being dependable. It made her a good researcher at jobs in college. It makes her good at keeping her kids' schooling and routines stable through international and interstate moves. And it makes her the friend I still call when I'm at odds with someone in my life. She has this knack for seeing and believing in the middle ground—the high ground—and doing whatever is needed to solve a problem.

But this collection of wonder-filled weirdness also creates natural enmity in her brain. How do you responsibly fix situations and not cause waves with people? How do you deal with communicating a strong and potentially unpopular belief *and* maintaining harmony with others? These are just two of the distinct strengths that Shannon is trying to balance.

It's no easy task to figure out which strength or quirk needs to take the lead in any given situation. But here are a few principles that can help us choose well.

First, what action shows love for God? Is there a scriptural principle for what I'm facing? How can it help me choose what best loves and honors God in this moment? If nothing comes to mind, commit the question to prayer, and look for wisdom as you read Scripture, listen to music, talk with friends, and walk through your day.

For my friend Shannon, this process might lead her to passages that clearly state what God expects her to do to love him and others most, such as 1 Corinthians 13 and Micah 6:8:

> He has told you, human one, what is good and
> what the Lord requires from you:
> to do justice, embrace faithful love,
> and walk humbly with your God.

Second, what action shows love for the other person right now? What can I do or say that would show he or she is important to me and that our relationship matters? What would honor the other person most? When the focus shifts from doing what we're best at to loving the people around us, it clears away the internal noise so we can fulfill the Greatest Commandment.

Shannon may need to look through her memories of times when people expressed they felt most loved by her and to live her strengths in the current situation just as she did then.

Third, what shows me love right now? Yes, we're here to love God and others. But if we're overstretched and overwhelmed and not taking good care of ourselves, we won't have the energy, emotionally or physically, to take care of others. It's the airplane safety instruction to put on your oxygen mask before you help someone else with his. When we don't turn our best parts toward ourselves as well as others, we become vulnerable to feeling overwhelmed, anxious, resentful, and depressed.

This principle may lead Shannon to find a quiet place to journal and listen to her body—to check in with her well-being and consider whether that's been accidentally sacrificed as she's lived her strengths and quirks.

For you or me, the process might look different. But however we approach these moments when our strengths and quirks fight among themselves, we can't ignore that internal struggle. If we do, our lack of action gives our weirdness's dark side permission to reign. We don't let our kids do that when they're fighting with their siblings. Why would we do that with the gifts that God has placed in our hearts?

> *When our strengths and quirks fight among themselves, we can't ignore that internal struggle. If we do, our lack of action gives our weirdness's dark side permission to reign.*

Consider your strengths and quirks. Which ones struggle to get along together? What are some classic trigger situations or relationships that invite the struggle?

31

WHEN THEIR QUIRKS RUB YOU THE WRONG WAY

When we take people . . . merely as they are,
we make them worse; when we treat them as
if they were what they should be,
we improve them as far as they can be improved.
—*Johann Wolfgang von Goethe,*
Wilhelm Meister's Apprenticeship

YEARS AGO, MY HUSBAND walked into the kitchen when he got home from work and said something that almost blew up our marriage: "Honey, let's rearrange the kitchen cabinets. What if we put the glasses in this one? And—"

The spatula whizzing by his face interrupted him.

Wiping my hair out of my new-mom, when-was-my-last-shower face, I took a mental inventory: dinner on the stove, preschool World Wrestling Federation ensuing, a crying baby wrapped in a sling around my torso, and the man wants to add a task to my life? His suggestion seemed so insensitive, so clueless, so hurtful to a mom of two then-foster kids who was still trying to figure out which way was up.

It was that tense place where my love for knowing and living our personal strengths was born. On the recommendation of a friend that same week, I'd done some reading and work to figure out my strengths.

Asking the right questions can take that relationship beyond survival mode to thriving mode.

And that's when the miracle happened: I realized my husband must have strengths too! (Yeah, I know. How can that be, with the comment about the cabinets?)

But it was true. And that moment—that realization—saved my marriage. It opened my eyes to the two questions that can make any relationship great: What strength is my partner trying to live right now? How can I see it so we're on the same team?

Goethe's quotation says it all: when we see people as they are (or as they appear to be, as was our case), we make them worse. But when we treat them as they should be—as if they're approaching us with good intentions—we help them become who they're capable of being. We give them a chance, in their weirdness, to be great. And we open our eyes to see God is at work in them.

When our quirks clash with someone else's, asking the right questions can take that relationship beyond survival mode to thriving mode. In my example, as I chose to see my husband's seemingly heartless comments for what they really were—his musing and thinking of ideas, a strength I've always loved in him—I could align with who he is at his best. Turning the conflict from him versus me to both of us trying to let each other live wonderfully drained the anger of the moment and left space for hope and joy.

What did that look like practically? To start, I had to figure out which one of my quirks was annoyed at which one of his. By following my resentment trail, I found the culprit. Each time he brainstormed ideas and shared them with me, I was automatically thinking, *I have to do that. Right now.* That response revealed the offended quirk: my "get 'er done" strength. It was mistranslating his think-of-ideas strength as a demand and a plan of action. On top of it all, my make-a-difference strength was offended because when he offered a suggestion for organizing the kitchen, I was hearing that as "You aren't a good organizer for our family." From there, away I went on the crazy train!

That's where the second step came in. I asked myself, *How can I see it so we're back on the same team?* Even asking the question put me in a posture of noticing and working with our commonalities instead of being run over by our differences. Turns out if I asked him, "Is this a fully baked [that is, get 'er done] idea? Or is it still pondering?" his ideas didn't get on my nerves nearly as often! It shocked me how many times he answered the latter, and I realized how often my get-it-done assumption was getting us in trouble. Over time, I learned to relax when he thought out loud, to see it as his mind and heart working as God designed: a beautiful gift of creativity and imagination (and gracious forgiveness for my hot-headedness!).

Some will read this and think, *No, this won't work. You don't understand. My partner has hurt me deeply. I can't give him the benefit of the doubt when we're in conflict.* It's true: none of us is good the way God is good (Mark 10:18). If your partner's choices and behavior aren't lined up with God's heart, you may have to approach the relationship cautiously. But that doesn't need to stop you from thinking in line with these questions. It just might mean that being on his team means holding the line with some strong boundaries and natural consequences for his behavior.

In the rest of your relationships, these ideas might just renew a friendship, open communication, or unlock the connections for which you long. For those benefits, isn't it worth holding off throwing that spatula long enough to ask these questions that help the "yours, mine, and ours" weirdness to be wonderful together?

Think of a recent conflict you've had with someone. What weirdness might he or she have been trying to live wonderfully?

32

WHEN YOU WISH YOU HAD
"BETTER" QUIRKS

NOTHER TIME WE GET stuck is when our strengths or quirks seem defective, weak, or unimportant in the grand scheme of things. Part of this skewed perspective comes from what we hear. Lots of personal growth material energizes and inspires us to dream and live differently, more boldly. But it also unwittingly creates a culture that puts far too much emphasis on the dynamic, influential, and productive strengths. I've seen this cause individuals with quieter or less publicly praised strengths and quirks to feel as though their gifts aren't good enough or that they're unimportant. That's a recipe for spending a lot of precious energy neglecting our unique design in favor of trying to behave like someone else we believe is making a bigger difference.

This is true for Cathy, a dear friend and one of my mentors as a mom and communicator. Cathy laments her seeming "propensity to waste time." Probably most of us would agree with her—wasting time really can be a weakness. We're supposed to make "the most of every opportunity" (Colossians 4:5) and work diligently at what we do if we want to be fulfilled (Proverbs 10:4). But what if what she's struggling with is not wasting time? What if the fact that her schedule's not full is actually what God wants for her?

When I asked Cathy whether she's seen her laid-back nature yield benefits, she admitted she had "seen the Lord, again and again, take my tendency to wander through my day to put me at the right place at the right time to minister to someone, to find a 'lost' soul—sometimes literally—and to help someone along the way." She also admitted, "My daughter-in-love tells me I have the gift of availability. Others tell me I am a 'Mary,' not a 'Martha' [Luke 10:38-42]. And my hubby often reminds me that I care more about people than housework, projects, and schedules."

Anyone else see wonderful in her weird? We'd be blind not to! But that's the thing about quiet strengths and quirks: we often don't look long enough to appreciate them. It's a myopathy in our society that leaves those with strengths like Cathy's to struggle intensely with a passage like the one found in Matthew 25, where Jesus shared a parable of servants entrusted with resources from their master before he departs on a journey. Each servant does what he feels best with his portion of the money while the master is away. When the master returns, he evaluates the servants' faithfulness with what he'd entrusted to them, and the ones who'd invested wisely, earning interest, get the master's praise. The master harshly rebukes the servant who buried what the master gave him, and the master sends him away.

Cathy says, "When I read that passage, it strikes me that the master calls the servant not only lazy but wicked! I hope with all my heart that I am able to stand before the Lord and at least return my talent with interest, if not multiplied back to him many times over. I wish there were more 'fruit' to show in my life."

First, let's take a good hard look at the "fruit" in her life: independent grown kids, grandkids she visits regularly. She speaks at retreats, teaches classes at church, and writes several blogs on family and faith. Those are facts you could itemize on a life résumé, the kinds of accomplishments we like to read about in the everyday hero stories in our favorite magazines. But it's what you wouldn't write on a résumé—her availability—that makes her a trusted advisor, a well-loved member of the church community, and the kind of person you want to hug whenever you see her.

Sometimes we're so biased against the value of our own strengths or quirks that we need objective insight to set us straight.

Just because you won't see the "gift of availability" listed on someone's curriculum vitae or in lists of spiritual gifts doesn't mean the one with that gift has done less with her life than the one who starts a nonprofit, shuttles refugees out of a war-torn nation, or discovers the cure for a disease. While the quieter strengths and quirks may not need the same balance and God-empowering as the louder, higher-visibility strengths, they're just as valuable as any others. These quiet quirks and strengths lie in the intangible, invisible but crucial realm of presence, community, and people development. These qualities honor the Greatest Commandment as much as the gifts that draw more attention because they, at their core, make space for loving people.

Appreciating our quieter strengths asks us to ponder, as I challenged my friend to do, the question: *What benefits has this quieter quirk brought me or others?* And it asks us to linger long enough for our hearts to answer honestly. It may even require us to ask others because, as Cathy's example shows, sometimes we're so biased against the value of our own strengths or quirks that we need objective insight to set us straight.

Perhaps you wonder, *Is it worth all that effort to discover value in a strength or quirk I'm not sure I even like?* I respond: Is it worth what you'll lose—those lives and hearts you won't touch—if you don't do that work?

Something to consider, no?

Whatever it takes, we can't forget about our quieter strengths. We've got to set our intention to learn about the wide variety of strengths out there—the "doing" strengths and the "being" ones—so we can gain confidence to succeed at doing what we naturally do and how we interact and love others best.

Do you know someone like Cathy? How might you encourage that person in his or her quieter quirks' immense value today?

33

WHEN ONE OF YOUR
QUIRKS IS TOO LOUD

NO ONE HAS JUST ONE quirk or weirdness. We're blessed (ahem) with a whole handful of them, and not all of these traits carry the same weight in our experiences. I mentioned my scoliosis earlier. That's a physical weirdness I manage and live with, but honestly, if my spine isn't whacked out of alignment on a given day, I forget I even have that issue. My "get 'er done now" tendency, however, isn't as easy to set aside. It's there when I'm trying to get the kids ready to leave the house. It's there when I have a deadline or project due. It doesn't discriminate between "being" moments and "doing" moments. And it often barges in, uninvited, when I least want it around, such as when I'm on vacation or when I'd like to fall asleep.

We all have quirks that seem more prominent than the others. These extra-loud quirks make up the lion's share of our unique design and how it shows up in our day-to-day lives. They're also the traits that come to mind first when someone asks what we'd like to change about ourselves. To avoid letting that one quirk bully our others out of their rightful places, it helps to look at real-life examples of how to keep these heavy hitters balanced with the others. How we manage a bossy quirk determines the amount of wonderful that shines through our weirdness.

Let's start with an example quirk I've often seen as a coach: responsibility. Because coaching is about living into God's best for our lives, I've noticed many of my clients have a strong sense of responsibility. They want to do the right thing, and they want to do it well—clearly very good motivations. But when "right" isn't a black-or-white answer, and when it's unclear how well is "well enough," those with a naturally strong sense of responsibility get tangled in a web of frustration, resentment, and procrastination.

Nina is no exception. What drives her quirk? The sense that she's "expected to do too much when others can or should just step up to their own tasks." Nina frequently takes on others' responsibilities too. One way she's found to manage this quirk is to wait before taking on another task when she's already overloaded. She gives others time to take care of the same needs she finds. Procrastination, so to speak, has become one of the ways she gives herself permission to sit back and let other people be responsible as well. Having worked with many clients who have strong responsibility traits, I've seen that procrastination is just one of many quirky ways to manage this drive to be responsible for every task in a five-mile radius.

Responsibility doesn't just show up in what we feel we must accomplish or take on. It also pops up, as my friend Laurie describes, as a "need to be seen as competent, even in things that I would have no reason to be competent in." She explained some benefits of this tendency: "[This quirk was] great if I was in your work group because, coupled with my hyper sense of responsibility, I would thoroughly research and stay up all night to complete a task well. However, I would also often bite off things that I had no business undertaking, like big home-improvement projects or large-scale projects like cooking lunch for seventy-five every Wednesday for seven weeks—in an apartment-sized kitchen with a newlywed's assortment of pots and pans."

I just love the heart in her words here. We need people with this sense of commitment and willingness to do what needs to get done. What we don't need, though, is for this tendency to chew up and spit out the people who have it.

How can a person so naturally gifted at being responsible and dependable keep from letting this strength become the eight-hundred-pound gorilla of doom in her life? She can begin by realizing there's a difference between what's needed and what she needs to do about it. She can give herself permission to let others take responsibility for some of the needs she recognizes. And she can allow herself to manage her own responsibilities imperfectly. A good friend once told me a great motto for those with loud responsibility and achievement strengths: Learn to get a B—in tasks and maybe even in life—instead of pursuing an A as though it rests solely on your shoulders. This rethinking allows Laurie, Nina, and anyone else struggling with an overbearing tendency to put it in perspective.

The basic idea with our too-loud strengths is this: when we're feeling bullied by one of them, we take a step back, consider how God reveals that trait, and use it more the way God would. For example, when empathy is turning to hypersensitivity, grumpiness, and exhaustion, we can look at how God reveals empathy. Jesus had compassion on people everywhere he went, but Jesus also completely removed himself from them for a regular recharge (Mark 1:35). If our overbearing strength is brainstorming, and it consistently robs us of a night's sleep, we follow God's example during the most dynamic brainstorming moment in history: the Creation. Even God, the most innovative, idea-generating being in the universe, made the choice to call it a day and celebrate the good things he'd created (Genesis 2:3).

If it's hard to find a scriptural passage that explicitly addresses God's use of traits that are too loud in our lives, we can look to other people who use those same quirks well. It takes a little effort to find them sometimes, but when you do, it's great for the soul! Remember that quirk I have? The one where I need to go after the big fish in life and invest in big projects with wide, public results? Honestly, as a Christian, it's hard to find examples of how to do this well (since humility is often equated with intentionally restricting this kind of desire). But as an excellent example, I discovered Blake Mycoskie, the founder and "Chief Shoe Giver" of TOMS Shoes. TOMS initiated the One for One model, which has provided more than two million pairs of free shoes to impoverished children worldwide since 2006. Even if the fruit of my strengths and quirks probably won't be shoes, I can read about how Blake developed his strengths to get ideas for how to grow my own.

We're not alone in our weirdness, as much as we feel that way at times.

The other benefit in learning and messing up with our loudest quirks is the relationships it can foster with people with similar quirks. Case in point: my friend Terra. Like me, she is a get-it-done girl. She has high standards for herself and others. I speak get-it-done-ese, and so we became natural friends from the start. I can help her find balance better than most because I see her more clearly than people who don't struggle with overachieving and being type A personalities the way we do.

Our friendship reveals to each of us the power of a community of people seeking to live the wonderful in our weirdness. It reminds us that we're not alone in our weirdness, as much as we feel that way at times. And it allows us to live 2 Corinthians 1:4, which says God "comforts us in all our trouble so that we can comfort other people who are in every kind of trouble. We offer the same comfort that we ourselves received from God." Perhaps that's what Paul meant when he wrote about traits that we consider less honorable—possibly referring here to our quirks:

> The parts of the body that people think are the weakest are the most necessary. The parts of the body that we think are less honorable are

the ones we honor the most. The private parts of our body that aren't presentable are the ones that are given the most dignity. The parts of our body that are presentable don't need this. But God has put the body together, giving greater honor to the part with less honor so that there won't be division in the body and so the parts might have mutual concern for each other. If one part suffers, all the parts suffer with it; if one part gets the glory, all the parts celebrate with it. (1 Corinthians 12:22-26)

Our weirdness often seems like the least presentable thing about us. But it's an opening for God's presence, power, and honor in ways our most-presentable traits can never be. Not because our strengths are depraved or selfish but because even our best is darkness in the presence of the light of the world. As we rest in all of who we are—strengths and needier quirks alike—and in the community of the other weirdos ordained to be in our lives, we unlock a sense of belonging and joy that nothing can snuff out.

Who do you know that "gets" you in your strongest quirks? What has that relationship taught you about honoring who God has made you to be?

34

WHEN WE CAN'T DO IT ALL

I CAN DO ALL THINGS THROUGH Christ who strengthens me" (Philippians 4:13 NKJV). When I read these words of the Apostle Paul, I tumble through a roller coaster of familiar emotions. At first the words breathe power into me. But then, almost as quickly, I deflate. What about those times I couldn't do all things? What about those times when everything worked out badly, even though my heart and intentions were aligned with what I believed God wanted me to do? What does God really mean in conveying this idea in Scripture?

If we go through enough tough stuff in life—struggle long enough with our quirks—even our strongest beliefs can start to crumble. But this verse gives us something to hold onto in those moments. Taking a deeper look allows us to recognize and appropriate what this familiar verse is trying to convey. And maybe even reveal something we've missed in the many readings of it through time.

What "I can do all things" *doesn't* mean:

- Doing too much. Being able to "do all things" doesn't mean we need to tackle them all at once. As a dear friend expressed it recently, we have to "keep the overbooker in us on a tight leash."

- Doing other people's work. Certain things are ours to do, and other tasks belong to those around us. We must set and maintain boundaries and focus our time, attention, and energy on those responsibilities that are ours alone.
- Doing whatever we want. Some activities are good and others less so or not at all; we need to exercise a little strategic vision and listen to our hearts. "A person without self-control / is like a breached city, one with no walls" (Proverbs 25:28). How powerless does that sound?
- Doing the same thing forever and ever, amen—especially if it isn't working any longer. Periodically reevaluate what you're doing with your time and heart to make sure it's still what you're meant to be doing and what's best for you. God didn't design us to pretend to be people we're not, to please everyone around us, or to be narcissists or victims.

What "I can do all things" *does* mean: in the original language the verbiage translates more like "I have the power and strength in me to do each and every individual thing that comes at me in this life . . . because of God's power and strength in me." That's some promise, isn't it? Its implications are that we can

- face any task—in God's strength;
- be confident in any circumstance—in God's strength;
- speak and listen in any conversation—in God's strength;
- overcome any fear—in God's strength;
- grieve and seek healing—in God's strength;
- embrace joy—in God's strength.

In God's strength, we can welcome any gift, press into hope, make the most of every experience, and bounce back from any loss. By God's strength, we can keep our weirdness in check, let God's wonder shine through, and know the abundant life God promises.

Now it's your turn. We've discussed many ways to appropriate these truths in the pages of this book. How will you walk forward from here into living your wonder-filled weirdness?

WEIRDNESS AND WONDER CHEAT SHEET
(THE DARK AND LIFE SIDES OF COMMON QUIRKS)

Trait	Dark Side(s)	Life Side(s)
achiever	perfectionist, focuses on tasks not relationships, fears failure	gets things done, hard worker, high standards
empathetic	moody, overly sensitive	understanding, relatable
responsible	overwhelmed, judgmental, perfectionist	reliable, trustworthy, moral
easygoing	lazy, unmotivated, ambivalent	adaptable, open to possibilities
analytical	indecisive (analysis paralysis), focuses on facts over feelings	detail oriented, looks at all the variables, good planner
organized	rigid, focus is on tasks not people	creates systems and plans, maximizes time and space, simplifies things
diplomatic	people-pleaser, controlling, codependent	brings harmony, helps resolve conflict and restore relationships
competitive	wants to win to the exclusion of others, makes others feel inadequate	high standards, brings about team or causes successes, catalyzes people to reach goals

Trait	Dark Side(s)	Life Side(s)
gregarious	dominates conversations, center of attention, may seem shallow in relationships	life of the party, networker, greeter, hospitable
commanding	bossy, demanding, "my way's the best way"	takes charge, mobilizes groups toward a goal, leader
communicator	talks too much, nitpicky with words, manipulative	connects with audiences, good marketer, conveys messages or ideas well to broader group
positivity	head in the clouds, unrealistic, naive	inspirational, uplifting, hopeful
idea generator	mind is frequently "someplace else," trouble settling on and executing ideas, seems flaky	open-minded, creative, curious, out-of-the-box thinker
confident	proud, arrogant	self-assured, builds confidence in others
strategic	slow to act, thinks too much, killjoy	well-thought-out ideas, planner, prepared

Author's Note

YOU'VE WORKED THROUGH THIS BOOK and made choices to spend your time here for a brief season. The enemy would love to see the work you've done here become a distant, ineffective memory. Don't let that happen! Take a stand and make the choice today to keep moving forward. Wherever you are in your journey, will you take at least one of these steps today?

Consider these questions:

- What idea most challenged me in this book?
- What more do I want to learn about my strengths or quirks?
- Finish this sentence: *In five years, I hope I'm . . .* What are some words you hope will describe you at your quirky best?
- What needs to happen in your life for you to get to that point? Create some goals.

Connect with a friend or your pastor to let him or her know what you're learning and where you feel God's leading you next.

Subscribe (http://eepurl.com/dovSD) to receive blog posts delivered free to your inbox, with tips and other resources to put this great stuff into practice!

AUTHOR'S NOTE

Join the community at www.facebook.com/LivingPowerLifeCoaching, where you'll receive daily inspiration, quotations, and coaching tools.

E-mail me (LaurieWallin@gmail.com) to set up your free thirty-minute coaching session and start moving toward confident, joy-filled living.

I'd love to help you step fully into who God designed you uniquely to be. As a coach, I've helped clients worldwide to save time, energy, and frustration by helping them (re)discover their strengths and passions, regain health and balance, and pursue dreams. I'd be honored to support you in pressing into all God has for you and your family.

Looking forward to helping you live with joy and confidence, no matter what life brings your way!

Laurie Wallin

Acknowledgments

No one can whistle a symphony.
It takes a whole orchestra to play it.
—H. E. Luccock

HUGE THANKS AND HUGS TO THE longtime dear friends in our home group. You've buoyed me in the toughest seasons and encouraged this book into existence.
And thanks to

- my pastor, Ken Hoelscher, for helping me be strategic about what I speak and write; and to Karla, my friend and sister, for her unending encouragement;
- Suzie Eller and Laura Polk, who inspired me to grow as a speaker by putting my heart on a page;
- my agent, Karen Neumair, for the ways she encourages and supports me as an author, despite my occasionally harebrained ideas;
- Donna Huisjen, who wasn't afraid to tackle a new author's writing;
- Lil Copan, Holly Halverson, and the entire team at Abingdon Press, for their gracious, insightful, and encouraging partnership in this process;
- those who courageously shared stories of struggles with their quirks so we could all learn and grow;

ACKNOWLEDGMENTS

- the amazing men and women on my prayer team who have labored alongside me for this whole project;
- my brother, who helped me find my kick-in-the-pants voice when I was drowning in what I "should" write;
- my sister, who helped me realize this book was meant to be, and who never shies from offering honest, life-giving feedback;
- my daughters, who've prayed, snuggled, and shared their mom with this book for a year;
- my husband, Gary, who listened to all my ideas—even at 1 a.m.— and who helped me to be strategic instead of living on the fumes of impulse.

And deepest thanks to my mom, dad, and stepdad, who for as long as I can remember have lived and spoken the message of this book into my life.

NOTES

1. To Question Our Quirks

Authors Albert Winseman . . . serve God and the world.

Albert L. Winseman, Donald O. Clifton, and Curt Liesveld, *Living Your Strengths: Discover Your God-given Talents and Inspire Your Community* (New York: Gallup, 2003), 1–2.

"Weakness," . . . would have us believe.

Blue Letter Bible, Greek *astheneia* (weakness), www.blueletterbible.org /lang/lexicon/lexicon.cfm?Strongs=G769&t=NKJV.

"The quickest way . . . comes to sunrise."

Ruth Graham, Jerry Sittser, and Joni Eareckson Tada, *When Your Rope Breaks* (Grand Rapids, Mich.: Zondervan, 2009), 56.

2. To Be Loved, Quirks and All

Weird: it's definitely . . . idea of worth.

Dictionary.com, s.v. "weird," http://dictionary.reference.com/browse /weird?s=t.

The increase . . . disenchanted world.

"Bullying," Facts for Families No. 80, American Academy of Child & Adolescent Psychiatry, March 2011, www.aacap.org/cs/root /facts_for_families/bullying.

"We're all . . . true love."

True Love: Stories Told to and by Robert Fuhlgum (New York: HarperCollins, 1998), 114–15.

"Christ's pursuit . . . anything else."
Emily P. Freeman, "A Million Little Ways," Chatting at the Sky, March 6, 2013, www.chattingatthesky.com/2013/03/06/a-million-little-ways/.

4. To Live Weird with (Not for) God

Young expresses . . . "[By doing] . . . with our love."
William Paul Young, *The Shack* (Newbury Park, Calif.: Windblown Media, 2007), 175.
God loves . . . character of God.
William Paul Young, "Creativity and the Writer's Identity: Worlds Colliding," September 21, 2012. Lecture, Re:write 2012, San Diego, California.

5. To Feed Your Best Weirdness

In his book . . . "You cannot . . . your heart."
John Eldredge, *Waking the Dead: The Glory of a Heart Fully Alive* (Nashville, Tenn.: Thomas Nelson, 2003), 88.
[i]It's the principle . . . "The one I feed."[/i]
"Native American Legends: Two Wolves," First People--The Legend, www.firstpeople.us/FP-Html-Legends/TwoWolves-Cherokee.html.
In the original . . . "to have . . . opinion of self."
Blue Letter Bible, Greek *phroneō*, www.blueletterbible.org/lang/lexicon/lexicon.cfm?Strongs=G5426&t=NIV.

6: Wrestling with Quirks

"So maybe, . . . more freedom."
Mary DeMuth, "Oh That Pesky Overactive Conscience," Mary DeMuth—Your Life Uncaged, February 28, 2012, www.marydemuth.com/oh-that-pesky-overactive-conscience/.

7. Squashing Wonderless Self-Talk

That sounds . . . "drives . . . word combinations."
Albert L. Winseman, Donald O. Clifton, and Kurt Liesveld, *Living Your Strengths: Discover Your God-given Talents and Inspire Your Community* (New York: Gallup, 2003), 80.

Mary shared . . . communication
Mary DeMuth, "Are You an Achiever?" Mary DeMuth—Your Life Uncaged, March 25, 2013, www.marydemuth.com/are-you-an-achiever/.

9. Seeing the Dark and Life Sides of Your Weirdness

Asked to take . . . others' eyes.
Albert L. Winseman, Donald O. Clifton, and Kurt Liesveld, *Living Your Strengths: Discover Your God-given Talents and Inspire Your Community* (New York: Gallup, 2003), 215.

10. Trusting God with Your Quirky Heart

"He has not . . . sanctified soul."
Matthew Henry, Psalm 37, in *Matthew Henry Commentary on the Whole Bible (Concise)*, www.biblestudytools.com/commentaries/matthew-henry-concise/psalms/37.html.

11. Your Designer Quirks and the Three Rs of Life

These Fibonacci . . . ear.
Vi Hart, "Doodling in Math: Spirals, Fibonacci, and Being a Plant [1 of 3]," YouTube, December 21, 2011, www.youtube.com/watch?v=ahXIMUkSXX0.
Let's unlock . . . Bible study.
Rick Warren, "A Simple Way to Unlock the Bible," Daily Hope with Rick Warren, January 26, 2012, http://purposedriven.com/blogs/dailyhope/?contentid=9977.

12. Your Wonderful and Why It Matters to the World

"Many evangelicals . . . is inaccurate."
Mark Driscoll, "5 Reasons Why Esther May Be the Toughest Bible Book I've Ever Preached," September 4, 2012, http://pastormark.tv/2012/09/04/5-reasons-why-esther-may-be-the-toughest-bible-book-ive-ever-preached.
"[spent] around . . . other women."
Ibid.

13. Your Tools for Living Strengths with Confidence

Brian Regan . . . someone else's!).
Brian Regan, "Standing Up," YouTube.com, 2007, http://www.youtube
.com/watch?v=zVRVA3mun3Q.

Part IV: Digging Deeper into Your Wonderful

Swept . . . before and nothing was found.
"Story of Staffordshire Hoard to be retold in new touring exhibition,"
www.staffordshirehoard.org.uk/news/story-of-staffordshire-hoard-to-be
-retold-in-new-touring-exhibition-2.
Two hundred forty bags . . . lives forever.
"Staffordshire Hoard," www.staffordshirehoard.org.uk/; Kevin Leahy,
"The Contents of the Hoard," http://finds.org.uk/staffshoardsymposium
/papers/kevinleahy.

16. Following the Leader Toward Wonderful

author Richard Swenson . . . anything well!
Richard Swenson, *Margin: Restoring Emotional, Physical, Financial and
Time Reserves to Overloaded Lives* (Colorado Springs, Colo.: NavPress,
2004), 17.

18. Learning from Some of History's Best-Known Weirdos

"the worst trouble . . . him of this."
"Notes on Arthur E. Morgan's first trip—Jasper [Arkansas, February
1909]," Morgan Papers, Library of Congress.
This bluntness . . . Gettysburg Address.
The Gettysburg Address, Avalon Project, http://avalon.law.yale
.edu/19th_century/gettyb.asp.
Randall E. Stross . . . "wheeler-dealer."
Randall E. Stross, introduction, in *The Wizard of Menlo Park: How
Thomas Alva Edison Invented the Modern World* (New York: Three Rivers,
2007), 3–4.
Edison also had . . . you guessed it: electricity.
Ibid., 7.

Another innovator . . . care of others.

Elizabeth Brown Pryor, *Clara Barton, Professional Angel*, Studies in Health, Illness, and Caregiving (Philadelphia: University of Pennsylvania Press, 1987).

In order to be . . . close relationships.

Ibid.

This woman . . . responsibility strengths.

Ibid., xii.

20. Riding the Sleep Train to Wonderful

We all know . . . worse moods.

R. Morgan Griffin, "Sleep: Moms and Sleep Deprivation," WebMD, March 17, 2010, www.webmd.com/sleep-disorders/sleep-benefits-10 /moms-sleep?page=2.

Adequate sleep . . . fighting chance.

Michael J. Breus, "Your Brain on Sleep," WebMD Expert Blogs, February 14, 2012, http://blogs.webmd.com/sleep-disorders/2012/02/your-brain-on -sleep.html.

21. The Differences Between Weirdness and Weaknesses

Unlike our . . . strongest ones.

Gal Chechik, Isaac Meilijison, and Eytan Ruppin, "Neuronal Regulation: A Mechanism for Synaptic Pruning During Brain Maturation," *Neural Computation* 11, no. 8 (1999): 2061–80.

Author and life . . . "Our divinely . . . much of anything."

Holley Gerth, *You're Already Amazing: Embracing Who You Are, Becoming All God Created You to Be* (Grand Rapids, Mich.: Revell, 2012), 27.

Shannon Cassidy . . . "Just stop . . . anyone notices."

Shannon Cassidy, "Leverage Leadership Strengths," in Steven Covey, et al., *Discover Your Inner Strength* (Sevierville, Tenn.: Insight Publishing, 2009), Kindle Edition.

Shannon goes . . . "Some tasks . . . serve a purpose."

Ibid.

I recently watched . . . "Weakness . . . is the way."

"J. I. Packer: Weakness Is the Way," Church Leaders—Lead Better Every

Day, www.churchleaders.com/pastors/videos-for-pastors/167043-j-i-packer
-weakness-is-the-way.html.

22. The Invisible Battle Behind Your Weirdness

One of my favorite . . . Do You See?
Bill Martin Jr. and Eric Carle, *Brown Bear, Brown Bear, What Do You See?*
(New York: Henry Holt and Company, 1995).
Author and inspirer . . . "The reason . . . brutal war."
John Eldredge, *Waking the Dead: The Glory of a Heart Fully Alive*
(Nashville: Thomas Nelson, 2003), 14.
In his book . . . "War is . . . restoration."
Ibid., 16.
John then shares . . . "Until we . . . and to us"
Ibid., 17.

24. The Way to Prevent Quirks from Becoming Weaknesses

I smacked into . . . "Any strength overdone is a weakness."
Shannon Cassidy, "Leverage Leadership Strengths," in Steven Covey,
et al., *Discover Your Inner Strength* (Sevierville, Tenn.: Insight Publishing,
2009), Kindle Edition.
What exactly . . . vision, right?
J. Vernon McGee. *Through the Bible with J. Vernon McGee*, vol. 5, *1
Corinthians—Revelation* (Nashville: Thomas Nelson, 1983), 142.

Part VI: Bouncing Back from Wonder Busters

The original . . . "Do you . . . complete?"
Blue Letter Bible, Greek *thelō* (intend), definition for English "want," www
.blueletterbible.org/lang/lexicon/lexicon.cfm?Strongs=G2309&t=NKJV.
Ibid., Greek *ginomai* (to become), definition for English "to be,"
www.blueletterbible.org/lang/lexicon/lexicon.cfm?Strongs=G1096
&t=NKJV.
Ibid., Greek *hygiēs* (whole, complete), definition for English "well,"
www.blueletterbible.org/lang/lexicon/lexicon.cfm?Strongs=G5199
&t=NKJV.

25. Using Mistakes to Shift Weird into Wonderful

"The greatest . . . make one."
Elbert Hubbard, cited in Cate Howell and Michele Murphy, *Release Your Worries* (Wollombi, NSW, Australia: Exisle Publishing, 2011), 50.

26. Releasing Perfectionism's Grip on Your Quirks

teleios, *translated "perfect," conveys:*
Blue Letter Bible, Greek *teleios*, www.blueletterbible.org/lang/lexicon /lexicon.cfm?Strongs=G5046&t=NKJV..

27. Overcoming Fears to Live Quirks Well

In the original . . . "to strengthen . . . resolute."
Blue Letter Bible, Hebrew *chazaq*, www.blueletterbible.org/lang/lexicon/ lexicon.cfm?Strongs=H2388&t=NIV.
In the New Testament . . . dozens of times.
Ibid., Greek *stēkō*, www.blueletterbible.org/lang/lexicon/lexicon.cfm ?Strongs=G4739&t=NIV.
In the New Testament . . . (encourage).
Ibid., Greek *parakaleō*, www.blueletterbible.org/lang/lexicon/lexicon .cfm?Strongs=G3870&t=NIV.
Paraklētos . . . *"to encourage."*
Ibid., Greek *paraklētos*, www.blueletterbible.org/lang/lexicon/lexicon .cfm?Strongs=G3875&t=ESV.

28. Changing Your Rules to Let Wonder In

A rule . . . governs a situation or behavior.
Dictionary.com, s. v. "rule," http://dictionary.reference.com/browse /rule?s=t.

29. Discovering Wonder in . . . Discipline?

In the original . . . "inherent strength."
Blue Letter Bible, Greek *dynamis*, www.blueletterbible.org/lang/lexicon /lexicon.cfm?Strongs=G1411&t=ESV.

Part VII: Learning from Real-Life Weirdness and Wonder

The only path . . . not-yet-amazing.
Seth Godin, "Overcoming the Impossibility of Amazing," Seth Godin's Blog, May 24, 2013, http://sethgodin.typepad.com/seths_blog/2013/05 /overcoming-the-impossibility-of-amazing.html.

30. When Your Quirks Don't Play Nicely Together

It reminds me . . . "makes planning the day difficult."
E. B. White, cited in Rachel M. MacNair, ed., *Working for Peace* (Atascadero, Calif: Impact Publishing, 2006), 63. White is the author of *Charlotte's Web.*

33. When One of Your Quirks Is Too Loud

I've ended up . . . worldwide since 2006.
"Bio of Blake Mycoskie, the Founder and Chief Shoe Giver of TOMS Shoes," TOMS.com, www.toms.com/blakes-bio/l.

34. When We Can't Do It All

What "I can . . . strength in me."
Blue Letter Bible, Greek *ischyō* (power, strength), www.blueletterbible .org/lang/lexicon/lexicon.cfm?Strongs=G2480&t=NIV.

Ibid., Greek *pas* (each, individually and collectively), www.blueletter bible.org/lang/lexicon/lexicon.cfm?Strongs=G3956&t=NIV.

Ibid., Greek *en* (because of), www.blueletterbible.org/lang/lexicon /lexicon.cfm?Strongs=G1722&t=NIV.